STUDIES IN LANGUAGE

STUDIES IN LANGUAGE

Introductory Readings
in Transformational Linguistics

RODERICK A. JACOBS
University of California, San Diego

XEROX COLLEGE PUBLISHING
Lexington, Massachusetts/Toronto

Cover photo
Science Photo/Graphics Ltd.,
Roy A. Gallant

ISB Number: 0–536–00693–8

Library of Congress Catalog Card Number: 77–168713

Printed in the United States of America.

To Roscinda Nolasquez
and the Cupeño people
ne-peewim

Preface

This collection of articles about language and meaning is intended to open up to interested non-linguists some of the varied areas of activity that have become known as transformational linguistics. Some articles deal with syntax, to be sure, but not just the syntax of modern English. There are articles about the sound pattern of language, prose style, semantics, English orthography, historical syntax, dialects, adverbs in English, abstract verbs in French, and linguistic theory. The goal is to communicate in clear English some of the excitement of delving into human language as transformational linguists have done.

At the end of this book are articles by four guest authors, all members of the Department of Linguistics at the University of California at San Diego. Two of the articles summarize major activity in fields not adequately covered elsewhere in the book. Pamela Munro's "Syntax and Dialects" deals with a much neglected area of linguistics—dialect syntax. For years, linguists have used elaborate surveys to collect and classify an immense amount of information about allophones, the use of *bucket* instead of *pail*, etc. But little effort has been devoted to discovering and characterizing syntactic differences among the dialects of English. Pamela Munro's article discusses and analyzes some of the more recent and most interesting work on this subject. Paul Chapin's detailed survey and evaluation of work in linguistic semantics skillfully cover a very complex field. It is, to my knowledge, the only such guide available. While these two authors have each covered a broad area of the subject, the other two guest authors take a narrow area and investigate it in detail. Each of their articles is a carefully reasoned attempt to provide a well-motivated solution to an important yet highly restricted problem area of a grammar. S.-Y. Kuroda takes a very recalcitrant problem in syntax, the status of adverbs, and reduces some of it to order. Bernard Tranel looks at the rather puzzling French words *voici and voilà* and suggests rather improbably that they are verbs. Nevertheless the evidence is marshalled, major objections are faced head on, and by the end the improbable has become probable.

My own articles are, wherever possible, arranged not only according to the area of linguistics covered but also in gradated sequences; thus material from earlier papers can illuminate later ones. Since many of the papers were written for this volume, the sequence of articles can be used to greater benefit than is possible in most other collections.

RODERICK A. JACOBS

Contents

General Background

A Note on Traditional and Structuralist Grammar

The twentieth century has marked a shift in the method of studying language. In the nineteenth and early twentieth centuries, languages were studied in terms of their chronological development (**diachronic** study) or their cross-linguistic relationships (**comparative** study). Today these approaches have given way to the detailed study of a particular language as it is (or was) during a particular period of time (**synchronic** study). Diachronic study is still going on, of course, despite the major shift in focus. Actually, the distinction between diachronic and synchronic studies is partly artificial. For example, adequate study of the development of relative clause formation from Anglo-Saxon to Middle English depends first on a detailed knowledge of the way this construction worked within the grammars of the language at each stage and its relation to other constructions in syntax, that is synchronic study. The use of the term "stage" is an arbitrary, though useful, one. It implies that languages have static stages during which no changes occur, whereas in fact languages are constantly changing, sometimes almost imperceptibly, sometimes very noticeably. Moreover, at any given time we will find considerable variation within a language, depending not only on where it is spoken but also on the speaker's age, sociological level, and many other interacting factors.

The major linguistic advances in the nineteenth century were in comparative and diachronic study. Linguists began to work out rules to account for systematically recurring likenesses and differences in phonology (the sound patterns of languages), morphology (word formation from roots, prefixes, tense, aspect endings, etc.)

3

and, less frequently, syntax (the way sentences are put together). For languages whose similarities were too systematic and widespread to be the results of accident or borrowing, they postulated language "families" and sought, when no parent language was recorded, to work out the forms that the parent language might have possessed. The achievements of such men as Rask, Grimm, Humboldt, Schleicher, Sir William Jones, Paul, and many others using the comparative method are described in standard histories of linguistics.[1]

Much of this work was continued in the present century by such men as Edward Sapir and Leonard Bloomfield. A major achievement of the latter was in comparative and historical work on the Algonquian group of American-Indian languages, where he demonstrated that the comparative method, rigorously applied, worked beautifully for a group of languages quite different from those previously studied.

Of course work like this depended on there being considerable linguistic data. But deeper comparison was rarely possible because, for example, too little was known about the relationship of tense suffixes in some languages to independent verbs in other related languages, and too little was known about phonological processes in many languages or about relative clause formation in others. Before fundamental comparative and historical research could be undertaken, there had to be more knowledge about the particular grammars of language, that is more synchronic study. Comparing lists of words in several languages was not really enough. By the end of the nineteenth century English was the most widely spoken language in the world. Yet little study in depth had been made of English syntax. There were a number of short grammars, and a few longer ones, many of them texts for teaching English to foreigners or for improving the English of native speakers by establishing upper-class usage as a model. Sometimes these grammars contained inappropri-

---

[1]For example R. H. Robins, *A Short History of Linguistics* (London: Longmans, Green and Co., Ltd., 1967), pp. 164–192; F. P. Dinneen, *An Introduction to General Linguistics* (New York: Holt, Rinehart & Winston, 1967), pp. 176–190; W. P. Lehmann, *Historical Linguistics* (New York: Holt, Rinehart & Winston, 1963); and, best of all, Holger Pedersen, *The Discovery of Language* (Bloomington, Indiana: Indiana University Press, 1967).

ate classifications designed originally for Latin or Greek. Some of the descriptions, however, included quite useful and accurate information about English. Ben Jonson's *English Grammar* (1640) reveals both the merits and faults of such grammars.

Up until the 1950's the majority of school textbooks followed such a tradition, sometimes labeled **traditional school grammar.** But all such grammars were very sketchy. Sometimes they focused on abuses of rules rather than on the way the rules of English worked. Their judgments as to whether a particular usage was "good" or "bad" were often based on class prejudice, inadequately defined notions of logic, and an emphasis on the superiority of formal written English over the less formal spoken tongue.

The tradition was, however, considerably enriched, especially in the early part of this century, when Otto Jespersen, George Curme, C. T. Onions, Henry Sweet, E. Kruizinga, and other linguistic scholars started to write detailed English grammars. Jespersen's seven-volume *A Modern English Grammar*, published between 1909 and 1931, is perhaps the best existing English grammar, embodying a wealth of information and perceptive insights. In general such grammars were organized in a way not so different from the traditional school grammars referred to earlier. They have thus become known as **scholarly traditional grammars**. A **grammar** is an attempt to relate meaning to linguistic form in an insightful way. These grammars were often haphazardly organized, and they have since been rather unfairly criticized for using unscientific criteria and anecdotal methods in their contributions to our understanding of the form/meaning dichotomy. Not all the criticisms are undeserved, but it is revealing that today no competent transformational grammarian would dream of describing any major area of English syntax without consulting one of Jespersen's volumes at some point in his investigations.

At about the same time during the early twentieth century, a newer movement that grew out of the nineteenth century comparative tradition was becoming influential. The **structural** linguists, as they were called, viewed language as a finite system requiring "scientific" investigation, which to them meant excluding meaning as a means of classification and using only data that were physically observable. Written language was merely a secondary representation of "real" language, oral language. For the earlier comparativists a language was a system of linguistically significant sound units modifiable in certain sound contexts. They attempted to work out generalizations or rules as to how the modifications came about. The structuralists took this idea much further, postulating language as a set of linguistic levels ranging from the basic phonological ones to the morphological, syntactic, and perhaps semantic levels. The scientific way to handle a language was to start from the lowest level, cataloguing the individual phonemes, finite in number, and the contextually determined realizations of these phonemes. After this had been thoroughly done, the next task was the cataloguing and interrelating of the morphemes—the distributions of the roots, prefixes, infixes, suffixes, etc.—which were made up of the already analyzed phonemes. These morphemes were to be classified strictly on the basis of forms. Adjectives were not "describing words;" they were forms taking suffixes such as *-ish*, etc. and appearing before nouns or after the copula *be*. At the level of syntax, a description consisted of a classification of different sentence types—sentences with a Noun-Verb-Noun-Noun pattern, etc.

In the areas of phonology and morphology, the structural linguists made major contributions to the study of both well known and exotic languages. Moreover the best among them, linguists like Leonard Bloomfield, Eugene Nida, Kenneth Pike, Mary Haas, and H. A. Gleason, tended in their actual practice to depart intelligently and insightfully from the rigidity of their theoretical and methodological pronouncements. However, even when less rigidly applied, structuralist techniques were quite unable to handle the complex and subtle phenomena of syntactic behavior, which requires a considerably more powerful apparatus, one capable not only of accurate classification but also of capturing the insights and immense productivity of the native speaker. This is a vast enterprise—one for which current progress in **transformational grammar** represents only a small, though significant, step.

Indeed transformational grammar in its earlier manifestations was not so different conceptually from the practice (not the theory) of earlier structuralist grammarians. It brought back the old universal or "rational" grammar tradition combined with some of the best insights of scholarly traditional grammar. It has at times been, like its structuralist predecessors, too concerned with formalisms and complex theoretical machinery. This last, however, has been a major asset, since the transformationalists forced themselves to work out in detail theories capable of accounting for the infinite creativity of language.

This is not to say that the structuralist movement is dead. The old theoretical rigidity has been more or less abandoned, but men like Kenneth Pike are still doing important work, investigating exotic and sometimes fast-disappearing languages. Some have developed theoretical systems such as Pike's **tagnemic theory**, which seeks to combine within an ambitious theory of human behavior structuralist data-classification techniques and some of the greater power of transformations to show the syntactic processes of natural language. There have been a number of attempts, such as Sidney Lamb's **stratificational theory**, to produce a viable alternative to transformational work, but unfortunately they have been unproductive. I say unfortunately because a theory of language needs soundly based and productive competition to achieve its potential. At present, however, transformationalism is providing some rival theories within itself. We are again witnessing some of the exciting activity of linguistic thrust and parry that makes linguistics a live and exciting discipline.

Syntax

Linguistic Universals and Their Relevance to TESOL[1]

The more we learn about language, the more ignorant we find we are. The transformational explosion in the past decade has generated an incredible amount of research into English, exceeding both in quantity and quality that of any two earlier decades. But the result has been to make grammarians uneasily aware of vast quantities of linguistic facts, generalizations, properties, and rules that cannot easily be subsumed within any neat grammatical framework. So the apparently glib mention of "universals" in the title of this paper may seem somewhat presumptuous. Perhaps I should have used the term **linguistic tendencies**. But since all the evidence is never in and since exceptions are hard if not impossible to find for the ones I shall discuss, the term universals does not seem too risky.

The two fairly secure universals discussed here may appear rather obvious, but their consequences have been little explored or exploited in the teaching of English as a second language. The discussion involves considerable use of meaning not only as a route for determining deep structure but as being almost if not completely identical to deep structure. That is, semantics and syntax are treated as fundamentally interdependent. Chomsky's early claim that grammar is best formulated as "a self-contained study independent

SOURCE: This paper was originally presented at the TESOL Convention in 1969 and was first published in the *TESOL Quarterly*, June 1969. Reprinted with permission of Teachers of English to Speakers of Other Languages, Washington, D.C.

[1]Teachers of English to Speakers of Other Languages.

of semantics" now appears more of a holdover from the heydays of structural linguistics than a useful tenet underlying present work in transformational linguistics. McCawley[2] has claimed that selectional restrictions have little or no independent status in linguistics. These seem to be semantic constraints on the set of possible messages. Thus it is pointless to claim that a paranoid who says

My toothbrush is alive and is trying to kill me.

is not observing grammatical restrictions requiring animate subjects for *alive* and *trying*. The difference between his usage and ours corresponds exactly to a difference in beliefs regarding relationships with inanimate objects. As McCawley has pointed out, a man uttering a sentence like the example above should be referred to a psychiatric clinic, not to a remedial English course.

In practice, at least, deep structure is taken to be a semantic construct which should eventually turn out to be common to all languages. In deep structure are all the elements that make up the meaning of a sentence. Obviously not all the elements are physically represented in the surface form of a sentence in any language. Since, like the traditional grammarians, I find the "process" image the most revealing, I treat this as **deletion** and claim it as a universal process in human languages. Although there is much redundancy in human language, a full semantic representation would involve considerably more redundancy. Obviously there must be certain conditions for deletion or the hearer would never be able to fill in the appropriate missing elements of the content. My three-year-old son now says

I want me to go.

He is quite logical. He is the one to do the wanting—hence the first pronoun. He is the one to do the traveling—hence the second pronoun. Later he will learn that the second pronoun must be deleted. Since he already understands the adult version, this kind of deletion is at least part of his language competence and auditory performance. Notice that he has filled in the missing part of a paradigm:

---

[2]James D. McCawley, "Where Do Noun Phrases Come From?" in R. A. Jacobs and P. S. Rosenbaum, *Readings in English Transformational Grammar* (Lexington, Mass.: Xerox College Publishing, 1970).

*I want me to go.[3]
I want you to go.
I want him/her to go.
I want us to go.
I want you (people) to go.
I want them to go.

The verb *want* is now quite regular. It is followed by a proposition containing an accusative, serving as semantic subject of *go*, and an infinitive, serving as predicate of the proposition. It just happens that under certain conditions the accusative form may or must be deleted. What kind of conditions govern possible deletions? There are two major ones that have been found in any human language, ranging from the Yuman languages of the southwest United States to the Malay–Indonesian languages in the Far East. However, I shall here use English for my examples.

In the sentences

(1) Cinderella promised her sisters to clean her room.
(2) Cinderella ordered her sisters to clean her room.

the surface forms look much alike, but there are important differences in the semantic relationships. In the first sentence Cinderella does the promising and Cinderella is also the one to do the cleaning. Thus the first sentence means something like *Cinderella promised her sisters for Cinderella to clean her room.* The second *Cinderella* is redundant here and is deleted on the basis of identity with another noun phrase. (The *for* is deleted for different reasons although it was retained in earlier forms of the language.) In the second sentence, although Cinderella does the ordering, *her sisters* are the ones scheduled to do the cleaning. Thus the second sentence means, roughly, *Cinderella ordered her sisters for her sisters to clean her room.* Here the second *her sisters* is redundant and must be deleted. (Note that abbreviated formulas are not needed to express these insights.) The difference between the two sentences—the first having the *subjects* of both verbs identical, the second having the *object* of the main verb identical to the *subject* of the other verb—has some important consequences. For example, the passive transformation applies only where the identical elements are the main *object* and the lower *subject*:

---

[3]An asterisk precedes sentences that are ungrammatical.

*Her sisters were promised by Cinderella to clean her room.
Her sisters were ordered by Cinderella to clean her room.

The reasons for this are beyond the scope of this paper.

This kind of deletion under identity is also part of what we call **pronominalization**. Thus when both references to *Caesar* in the following sentence refer to different persons

Caesar admired Caesar in the mirror.

the sentence is correct. But when they refer to the same person, that is, when the identity condition applies, the second *Caesar* is deleted and replaced by a form having the same gender, number, and case interpretation but with the "proper-ness" removed, namely the reflexive pronoun *himself*.[4] The *-self* form, it should be noted, depends not just upon grammar but upon semantic reference.

In English, deletion under identity involves certain other properties which may not apply in some other languages and which are not as obvious as they might seem. We will take pronominalization and reference as an example. Assume that the pronoun *he* in each sentence refers *only* to Leif Eiriksson. In the following pairs of sentences, only the *a* sentences are acceptable:

(3)*a* Leif Eiriksson said that he was coming.
  b He said that Leif Eiriksson was coming.
(4)*a* Leif enjoyed exploring although he complained frequently.
  b He enjoyed exploring although Leif complained frequently.

This suggests that the "antecedent" of a pronoun must actually antecede. The question of distance between the antecedent and the pronoun seems to make little difference, as can be seen in

(5)*a* *Leif* claimed that the maiden who had asked the king to send the ship to Greenland although it was supposed to be sailing to Vinland had said that *he* was cute.

---

[4]For more detailed discussion, see Jacobs and Rosenbaum, *English Transformational Grammar* (1968) and *Transformations, Style, and Meaning* (1971), both from Xerox College Publishing, Lexington, Mass.

b *He claimed that the maiden who had asked the king to send the ship to Greenland although it was supposed to be sailing to Vinland had said that *Leif* was cute.

But it is not necessary for the "antecedent" to antecede:

(6) Although *they* enjoyed ravaging, *the Vikings* preferred mead-drinking.
(7) As soon as *he* entered, *Darcy* encountered coy female simpers.

It appears that if the pronoun is in a subordinate clause, it may precede its "antecedent." In fact, the situation is more complex, but this generalization applies fairly widely in English and, I believe, in most Indo-European languages.

I have perhaps implied that deletion applies only to noun phrases. But much the same process, called **gapping** by some grammarians, is noticeable in

(8)*a* Isabella *liked* potted plants and Lamia serpents.

The deleted verb in the second of the conjoined sentences can only be *liked*, a verb identical to the verb in the first part of the sentence. Note that deletion here applies only left to right.

(8)*b* *Isabella potted plants and Lamia *liked* serpents.

It has been claimed that this kind of deletion, gapping, is done left to right in languages where sentences have subject-verb-object ordering, and right-to-left where languages have subject-object-verb ordering. If this is indeed a universal, then presumably the equivalent of (8)*b* would be correct in an S-O-V language except that the verb meaning "liked" would be at the end of the sentence:

Isabella potted plants and Lamia serpents *liked*.

However, evidence from Samoan and some American Indian languages suggests at least that this "universal" may be just a "tendency."

So one main condition for deletion, identity, is probably a universal, although other properties involved vary among languages. Ideally, the teacher of English as a second language knows how identity deletion operates in the native languages (or dialects) of his pupils; in fact, such a situation is unlikely for some time.

The second condition for deletion involves indefinite elements in languages, for example, words like *anyone, someone, anything,* and *something* in English. Thus only the second sentence below

(9)*a* It is easy for Authun to please Sweyn.

b It is easy for anyone to please Sweyn.

can be paraphrased as

(9)*c* It is easy to please Sweyn.

Except when it is subject of a clause, an *indefinite* noun phrase may usually be deleted without affecting the basic meaning. This *indefiniteness* condition upon deletion is also believed to be universal.

When a noun phrase has been deleted either because it is identical to some other noun phrase or because it is an indefinite noun phrase like *anyone,* can the native speaker of English always tell which process has been applied? The following sentence suggests that without adequate context he cannot.

(10) The police were ordered to stop rioting in Chicago.

There are two principal interpretations here. One can be represented rather roughly as:

(10)*a* *The police were ordered for the police to stop rioting in Chicago.

The second "the police" is then deleted under identity. The other interpretation is approximately:

(10)*b* The police were ordered to stop anyone from rioting in the park.

The indefinite noun phrase "anyone" is deleted.

Normally native speakers have little trouble where deletion is involved. However, difficulties are likely to arise for non-native speakers, especially if their native languages are not Indo-European. The teacher must expect that deletion is a common process in whatever language his pupil speaks. He may wish to find out just how deletion in the other language resembles that in English and how it differs. When I taught Indonesian students I found that the deletion and relativization processes in that language were very similar to those in English. Once the students knew how English relative pronouns were like *jang* in Bahasa Indonesia, it was easier to show the differences and to teach correct usage. Similarly discussion of sentence embedding processes in the other language leads logically into understanding of the *that, for . . . to*, and *possessive . . . ing* complementizers in English used with embedded (or complement) sentences in English. Eventually the non-native speaker must, like the native speaker, know how these sentences happen to be basically synonymous.

> (11)*a* *That* Galahad had arrived early surprised Lancelot.
>   *b* *For* Galahad *to* have arrived early surprised Lancelot.
>   *c* Galahad*'s* hav*ing* arrived early surprised Lancelot.
>   *d* It surprised Lancelot *that* Galahad had arrived early.

In advocating more strongly comparative rather than just contrastive emphasis, I am suggesting that the likenesses between languages and even the universal characteristics are inadequately exploited. Moreover I am assuming that the "direct method" alone is likely to be inefficient. And, of course, I am wildly impractical. I seem to be assuming that teachers will know both a transformational grammar and also the relevant characteristics of the native languages of their students. Chemical-type formulas are far from necessary in any grammar although such abbreviations may be of use to theoretical linguists. Without the formulas, a good transformational grammar of English should be easily mastered, and its coverage of English is far more insightful than "mathematophobes" suspect. This does not mean returning to just teaching the "rules" of English. The existence of properties relevant to all or many languages, sometimes in quite detailed ways, has not been adequately exploited. And the teacher who doesn't speak the native language of his students should have a presently non-existent, simply written booklet, published by the Center for Applied Linguistics in the year 2270, which points out how each other language resembles and differs from English in the details of deletion, complementation, expression of quantification, relativization, conjunction, and so on. If a more insightful and more comprehensive framework than current transformational grammar is then available to linguists, the authors of the booklet will undoubtedly use it.

Recent developments in transformational linguistics itself suggest that progress is being made in a number of areas important to teachers of English as a second language. The fact that much of this work is being done in languages ranging from the Uto-Aztecan family to Finnish and Korean suggests that English is not being used as "a strait-jacket into which to force the structures of all other languages." For English-speaking linguists, however, it serves as the most convenient and best documented language on which to start testing hypotheses as to linguistic universals.

Recent Developments in Transformational Grammar

Noam Chomsky's pioneer book, *Syntactic Structures*, is now well into its second decade. Linguistics today is a very different field from linguistics in 1957, and it was this book that started the change. Chomsky succeeded in showing that earlier grammars of human languages were incapable of dealing with some of the most important properties of language. The sets of rules used could not account for the infinite set of sentences that makes up any human language. The empirical claims made by such grammars were limited by their format: listing of categories and items, procedures for cutting up sentences and so forth. Consequently such grammars could do little to help us understand the nature of a language system which could be learned so rapidly by small children, a system allowing infinite creativity to its users. The grammars, or rather fragments, since no one has yet written a full one—could not explain how native speakers understand expressions in one way rather than another, how they were able to make use of certain kinds of syntactic information not obviously present on the surface of sentences to interpret them correctly. Chomsky's vastly more powerful model of language included two principal levels of structure: a **deep structure** which in some not always precise manner embodied the meaning, and a **surface structure** which was the set of forms which are converted into sound or writing as the sentences of a language. The deep structure was a level produced (or generated) by a set of rules, called Phrase Structure Rules, enumerating the basic parts of a sentence. For example:

Sentence → Noun Phrase   Auxiliary   Verb Phrase

or

S → NP   AUX   VP

Then a set of **transformations**, some obligatory, some optional, converted these deep structures into surface structures. Certain very simple sentences to which only obligatory transformations had been applied were called **kernel sentences**. The transformations were not rules like the one illustrated above. Instead of expanding elements such as sentence, noun phrase, auxiliary, verb phrase into their component parts, transformations changed the structure of entire sentence units, deleting, substituting, and adjoining forms in a sentence structure. Earlier structural grammars had almost inevitably confined themselves to the less powerful phrase structure rules. Chomsky showed that only by using both kinds of rules could a grammar come close to making explicit what it is a native speaker knows about his native language.

One rather disarming characteristic of Chomsky's insistence on explicitness was that the principles and claims underlying his theory of language were clear and therefore open to challenge. These claims could be disproven by empirical investigation not only of many languages but also of psychology and neurology. *Syntactic Structures* set off explorations by generations of doctoral students and their professors of scores and scores of languages, of language acquisition by children, and especially of the English language, mother-tongue of most of the investigators. Among them was Chomsky himself, very much aware that the mystery of language was far from being solved.

As Chomsky saw, his first book, important though it was, suffered from a number of major defects. A grammar of any language written on the 1957 model would be precise but unwieldy. Moreover there were many areas of sentence formation, semantic relations, and lexical information which were not dealt with, or which were treated clumsily. Lexical items, for example, were introduced into deep structures by the same kind of phrase structure rules as those indicating the major constituents of a sentence. One rule isolated a group of verbs into a category "transitive verb." A subsequent one subcategorized transitive verbs into those which require animate subject noun phrases and those which don't. Then again this subcategory contained further subcategories of verbs which can take on the progressive aspect and those like *know* which cannot:

*Eric was not knowing Italian

and so on until there were hundreds, potentially thousands of categories, some perhaps containing a single verb. Worse still, some significant linguistic generalizations could not be expressed within this system because the categories were set up as hierarchies. Thus nouns are subdivided into common nouns and proper nouns. Each of these categories is separated into concrete and abstract subcategories. Thus *democracy* is a common abstract noun, *Buddhism* is a proper abstract noun, *Christopher Columbus* is a proper concrete noun whereas *lighthouse* is a common concrete noun. The categories influence the type of verb that occurs with them and the presence or absence of an article. But the choice between *who* and *which* in relative clauses is one of many indications that humanness and non-humanness are grammatically significant in English. So we further subdivide into animate and inanimate and then human and non-human. Thus the common concrete subcategory is separated into two others, one containing, for example, *cement, houses, books,* the other, *cow, doctor, tree-rat.* Then the common concrete animate nouns are further subdivided into human and non-human ones. The same kind of subdividing goes on in the proper noun category, since *Christopher Columbus* is a human noun which, like *doctor,* can be subject of a verb like *discuss,* be modified by *who* rather than *which,* and can, unlike *rock,* be the object of *murdered* (used nonfiguratively). The trouble is that there is no way to justify using common and proper as higher level categories rather than animate and inanimate. The above hierarchy provides a simple way to formulate rules about common and proper nouns. But there is no easy way to talk about the properties all *human* nouns share. Instead we have to talk about *common* etc. *human* nouns and *proper* etc. *human* nouns. The hierarchy could as easily be the other way round with *animate/inanimate* at the highest level. When the *mass/count* noun distinction is included, matters get worse.

Furthermore the notion of transformation in *Syntactic Structures* includes both meaning-preserving and meaning-changing processes. The passive rule, which simply provided a paraphrase for certain kinds of active sentences, is quite a different kind of operation from the negative transformation which converted an affirmative into its negation. If meaning-changing processes are allowed, then the deep structure cannot be the sole component for semantic interpretation. The emphasis laid upon *kernel* sentences is misleading. What is important is the more abstract set of basic relationships expressing such notions as who does what to whom and with what modifications. Relationships such as deep subject, object, predicate phrase, and relative clause underlie all sentences, not just kernels. The interrelationships of parts of complex sentences are unrepresentable in the deep structure. Instead they are produced by rules called *Generalized Transformations*. These are quite different from other transformations because they do not operate on a single sentence structure. Instead they combine artificially separate sentence structures. But since both subordination and co-ordination are very much a part of meaning, these notions should really be present in some fashion in the deep structure—if the deep structure is to represent basic meanings. After all

The boy wants it.

and

The boy goes home.

hardly mean the same as

The boy wants to go home.

Yet the basic insights—the fundamental notions of transformations, of a more abstract level of structure, of the recursive and creative properties of language, of the need for formal explicitness and of the kinds of empirical claims made in a formalized grammar—seemed, and still seem, sound. In the seven years following *Syntactic Structures*, the transformational grammarians worked to modify and improve their model of language, to expand and deepen its coverage of particular languages and to isolate the universal characteristics of human languages. Edward Klima showed how question transformations could be made meaning-preserving by including in the deep structures of questions an element signifying "it is a question whether," abbreviated as QUESTION or WH. Since this question element is part of the meaning of the sentence, the deep structure more adequately represented the meaning.

Moreover the symbol could be used to trigger the application of the question transformation. This shifts the auxiliary around the subject and replaces the question symbol. R.B. Lees put forward similar proposals for negative sentences. Gradually, and a little painfully, Chomsky, Klima, Postal, Lees, Rosenbaum and many others revised the notion of deep structure—indeed first gave it that name—so that it became a more abstract mental object embodying both the important earlier categories and relationships and also elements representing negation, command and interrogation. A deep structure could now be quite complex, revealing considerable subordination and coordination. Such a deep structure was now a little closer to the ideal of a deep structure common to all human languages which would reflect the innate properties of the human mind. It was no longer necessary to have meaning-changing transformations. The deep structure provided all the information necessary for interpretation by a semantic component of the grammar. Kernel sentences and generalized transformations disappeared from almost everywhere but public school textbooks. The complex subcategorization system was replaced by another in which the various characteristics of individual words, many of them idiosyncratic, could be represented as properties or features that were not in a hierarchy but were unordered in a part of the deep structure called the lexicon. In the lexicon were entries for individual words and morphemes, a little like dictionary entries except that they specified such properties as "takes an animate subject," "plural only" and "abstract." Since human beings do acquire this lexical information in this non-hierarchical manner, this seemed a better model. More importantly, this kind of lexicon could incorporate far more necessary information far more simply and intuitively than the earlier model. The basic subject, predicate and modifier relationships are previous to and separate from the lexicon. These are the aspects common to all languages.

The important book representing this rethinking about language is Chomsky's *Aspects of the Theory of Syntax* (1965). This and a number of more specialized books provided a firmer base for the more detailed exploration of languages, especially English.

But as linguists studied language in more depth than ever before, they found that the deep structure suggested in *Aspects* was still not adequate to represent some areas of meaning. Perhaps there

was a deeper level, one which needed no separate semantic component because it was itself the meaning. Already the basic synonymy of

> Garibaldi bought the alligator.
> The alligator was bought by Garibaldi.
> What Garibaldi bought was the alligator.
> It was Garibaldi who bought the alligator.

and, in important ways,

> for Garibaldi to have bought the alligator . . .
> Garibaldi's having bought the alligator . . .
> that Garibaldi had bought the alligator . . .

had been accounted for by postulating a common deep structure
together with transformations converting it into the various surface
structures. These transformations were all required not for just
these constructions but for many other areas of English syntax.
Sometimes they worked for other languages in much the same way.

But there were other instances where closely related and even
synonymous sentences came from very different deep structures.
Surely

> Garibaldi bought an alligator from Cedric.

and

> Cedric sold an alligator to Garibaldi.

are synonymous, though perhaps with a slight difference in focus.
Cedric is no less an *actor* than Garibaldi. The verb *bought* has in
common with *sold* the notion of a transfer probably for money.
The alligator goes *from* Cedric *to* Garibaldi. One verb stresses the
"from-ness," the other the "to-ness." Some highly influential work
by Jeffrey Gruber explored this in more detail. Verbs like *buy* which
contain a semantic notion plus *from* are quite common in English,
as are the *to* verbs. Here are a few others:

from	**to**
get	give
acquire	yield
receive	grant
borrow	lend
win	lose

Some verbs contain both:

transfer	shift
pass	carry
move	toss
push	lift
migrate	hasten

What Gruber and many others were seeking to do was to go below the *Aspects* deep structure to a semantic rock-bottom where the various semantic notions would be separated out. At this level the categories of words (verbs, nouns) would be irrelevant. Chomsky's deep structure contained transitive and intransitive verbs. In fact the distinction is unimportant further down. For example there are two verbs *roll*, one transitive, one intransitive.

> Jack rolled the egg towards the cliff.
> The egg rolled towards the cliff.

But the same notion of motion underlies both. The first sentence has an additional *causal* feature, which could be expressed separately.

> Jack caused the egg to roll towards the cliff.

This kind of semantic information thus has syntactic consequences. And motion verbs, like *roll,* and even *learn* are very different from the static verbs like *remain* and *know*. The former can always take the progressive (*be . . . ing*) forms, while the latter either don't take it at all or only do it when an animate subject is consciously causing the action.

> He is learning French.
> *He is knowing French.
> He is remaining in the room.
> *It is remaining in the room.

The work of Lakoff, Postal, Rosenbaum, Ross and others was showing that the surface structure parts of speech were not necessarily the best categories for the deeper structures. Lakoff showed that verbs and adjectives were basically the same kind of constituent in the deep structure. Of course many languages don't make the distinction even in the surface structure. In a brilliant paper, Postal showed that articles and pronouns were the same class at a deeper level and was thereby able to explain a number of mysteries in English syntax and dialect studies. This kind of research was gradually changing the underlying map of English grammar. In 1968 Jacobs and Rosenbaum's book, *English Transformational Grammar,* incorporated much of this work for a wider audience. Studies by Barbara Hall Partee, Lightner and others challenged the apparently fundamental notions of deep subjects and objects, for there seemed to be under them a semantic level containing more basic notions. Paradigms such as the following were used to show that deep subjects were not as deep as claimed:

(1) Someone broke the window with something.
(2) Something broke the window.
(3) The window broke.

Consider a set of semantic relations: **agent**, **object** and **instrument** (for *someone, the window* and *something* respectively). The first sentence uses all three categories with *broke.* If the noun phrase serving as agent is deleted, the instrument noun phrase can act as a subject. Hence the second sentence. If the instrument noun phrase is removed, then the object noun phrase becomes the subject. Hence the third sentence. From evidence like this, Fillmore, of Ohio State University, argued for going beneath the deep structure to a level where **cases** like agentive, instrumental and object expressed basic semantic relationships. The kinds of preposition, the actual forms of verbs, the type of noun (animate or inanimate, etc.), seemed to be influenced, in part controlled, by these deep deep structure cases. James McCawley, then at the University of Chicago, Paul Postal of IBM, Ross and Lakoff at Harvard and M.I.T., and many others tried to work out some ways of formulating a deep semantic structure, some using the notions of symbolic logic, others positing pro-forms like *cause-to-die* for *kill.* This kind of deep deep structure would be concerned with propositions rather than sentences. Consequently it would be a far more abstract level.

But with this deeper exploration came deeper problems. Too little is known yet about the nature of meaning, about what happens before a meaning "rises" to the approximate level, say of Chomsky's deep structure. In a recent and very important paper, "Remarks on Nominalization," Chomsky takes note of the various proposals and modifies his notion of the deep structure. Here base forms are not specified as nouns or verbs but have certain stated potentials for becoming one or more of these in the surface structure, for example *refuse* or *refusal*. With changes like this, Chomsky's model of language approaches still more closely the ideal of a universal deep structure.

But the explorations and questioning still go on as languages are more and more exhaustively analyzed. The present grammatical models can handle a vastly greater amount of data than the relatively simple model presented in *Syntactic Structures*. Yet in important respects the 1957 model and the 1969 models are much the same. The deep structure level, though not basically semantic, is still a highly useful one for describing important aspects of language and for serving as a base upon which major transformations may operate. Such investigations have told us more about the structure of English than has been learned over many centuries. But the essential mystery of language, the mystery that is at the heart of humanness, remains. Hopes for early solutions are still premature.

Select Bibliography

CHOMSKY, N. *Aspects of the Theory of Syntax.* Cambridge, Mass.: M.I.T. Press, 1965.

FILLMORE, C. J. "The Case for Case" in *Universals in Linguistic Theory.* New York: Holt, Rinehart & Winston, 1968.

———. "The Grammar of *Hitting* and *Breaking*" in Jacobs and Rosenbaum, *Readings*, 1970.

GRUBER, J. S. "Look and See," *Language*, Vol. 43 (1967), pp. 937–947.

———. *Functions of the Lexicon in Formal Descriptive Grammars.* Technical Memorandum 3770, System Development Corp., Santa Monica, California, 1967.

JACOBS, R. A. *On Transformational Grammar.* Monograph Series 11, New York State English Council, 1968.

JACOBS, R. A. and ROSENBAUM, P. S. *English Transformational Grammar.* Lexington, Mass.: Xerox College Publishing, 1968.

———. *Readings in English Transformational Grammar.* Lexington, Mass.: Xerox College Publishing, 1970.

———. *Transformations, Style, and Meaning.* Lexington, Mass.: Xerox College Publishing, 1971.

LAKOFF, G. *On the Nature of Syntactic Irregularity.* Cambridge, Mass.: M.I.T. Press, 1969.

LANGACKER, R.W. *Language and Its Structure.* New York: Harcourt Brace Jovanovich, 1967.

KLIMA, E.S. "Relatedness Between Grammatical Systems," *Language,* Vol. 40 (1964), pp. 1–21.

MCCAWLEY, J.D. "Where Do Noun Phrases Come From?" in Jacobs and Rosenbaum, *Readings,* 1970.

POSTAL, P.M. "On So-Called 'Pronouns' in English" in Jacobs and Rosenbaum, *Readings,* 1970.

ROSS, J.R. "On Declarative Sentences" in Jacobs and Rosenbaum, *Readings,* 1970.

Syntax and Meaning

A grammar of a language represents an attempt to relate the form of the utterances of a language to their meaning. This involves accounting for the kind of synonymy represented by:

(1) Moses foresaw the seven years of famine.
(2) The seven years of famine were foreseen by Moses.

and it involves accounting for the ambiguity of the following sentence:

(3) Entertaining guests can sometimes become wearisome.

It further involves accounting for the native speaker's awareness of what is a permissible sentence in his language and what is not, an awareness acquired gradually but early in his childhood. This awareness or implicit knowledge enables him to produce and understand utterances he may not have previously heard. Finally a grammar must provide an explanation of the native speaker's understanding of the semantic interrelations within a sentence. For example, the noun phrase *the messenger* is the logical *object* of *follow* in sentence (4) but the logical *subject* of *follow* in sentence (5):

(4) The messenger was not hard to follow.
(5) The messenger was not reluctant to follow.

The surface forms of the sentences seem almost identical in structure, the difference being that one uses the adjective *hard* while the other uses the adjective *reluctant*. But the difference in the underlying logical relationships correlates not just with the differing semantic readings for the two adjectives. In active sentences the normal position for objects is that just after the verb. In fact such a position is possible for a paraphrase of (4) but not for one of (5):

(6) It was not hard to follow the messenger.
(7) *It was not reluctant to follow the messenger.

similarly,

(8) To follow the messenger was not hard.

but not

(9) *To follow the messenger was not reluctant.

Thus, formal differences also match the meaning differences.
Now look at the following sentences:

(10) The messenger was not hard for anyone to follow.
(11) It was not hard for anyone to follow the messenger.
(12) For anyone to follow the messenger was not hard.

Note that none of the sentences above would be grammatical if I substituted *reluctant* for *hard*. Now sentences (10), (11) and (12) are not only paraphrases of each other but they are also paraphrases of (4), (6) and (8). In fact, remove *anyone* together with its subordinating marker *for* (usually labeled complementizer), and sentences (10), (11) and (12) are identical in form with sentences (4), (6) and (8), respectively.

One way for a transformational linguist to account for all this is for him to postulate a more abstract level of language, one which contains, for example, all the semantic content of sentences (4), (6), (8), (10), (11) and (12). At such a deep level, all six sentences would be a single structure. Then he has to account for the difference in the surface forms of the six sentences. To do this he must show what grammatical processes or "transformations" convert this deep structure into six different surface structures. However, if his grammar is to be anything more than an elaborate listing the linguist must show that the transformations he uses were not just invented to account for the six sentences alone. They must be fairly general processes of sentence formation in the language described.

A full deep structure would not consist of real words but of representations of meanings. So *kill* like *die* might be represented by some description involving the notion, "cease to live" but *kill* would differ from *die* in including an additional causative element. So if *die* means that someone ceases to live, *kill* means that someone causes someone to cease to live, probably by violent means. If the two "someones" refer to the same person, the notion can be represented by such phrasings as *kill himself* or *commit suicide*, while if they differ in reference and the dead person is an important figure, the verb *assassinate* can be drawn from the lexicon or vocabulary of the English language. Similarly *murder* involves a further complexity to do with criminal laws relating to different types of killing. Moreover a deep structure, if it really represents the semantic content, must also represent such semantic relations as *actor, object* and *instrument*. In the sentence:

(13) Shirley shattered the showcase with a shell.

these relations are quite clear. But, in fact, if the agent is not specified, the instrument can act as subject:

(14) A shell shattered the showcase.

while if the instrument is also unspecified, the logical object must be the subject:

(15) The showcase shattered.

Here again formal differences correlate with semantic differences.

Since so little is presently known about meaning, lexical or syntactic, the linguist describing the syntactic properties of the six sentences mentioned earlier would probably content himself with a labeled family-tree type diagram or even a string of words (both of which are merely abbreviations for the complex phenomena described above). For our purposes I shall posit the highly abbreviated structure:

(16) it/*for* anyone *to* follow the messenger/was not hard.

The "complementizers" or subordinating markers *for* and *to* are probably also the result of transformations. The words within the slashes / / are a "complement" or embedded sentence. Obviously some transformations must be applied even if this abbreviation is taken as the real deep structure. The word *it* does sometimes precede embedded sentences.

(17) He'll see to it/that you don't come here again/.
(18) I hate it/for you to talk to me like that/.

But the *it* (together with certain other words) can be deleted before a complement:

(19) He'll see/that you don't come here again/.
(20) I hate/you to talk like that/.

This needed "it-deletion" transformation can also be used to convert:

(16) it/for anyone to follow the messenger was not hard.

into the grammatical sentence:

(12) For anyone to follow the messenger was not hard.

Alternatively the *it* could be retained and the complement shifted to the end of the main sentence, yielding the grammatical sentence:

(11) It was not hard for anyone to follow the messenger.

This transformation is known as **extraposition**.

The underlying structure of sentences like:

(21) It was easy for anyone to please Janice.

can be transformed by taking the object of the embedded sentence and substituting it for the word *it*.

(22) Janice was easy for anyone to please.

The same "it-replacement" transformation can convert the extraposed structure (11) into:

(10) The messenger was not hard for anyone to follow.

Thus sentences (10), (11) and (12) have been linked to the deep structure (16) by transformations already necessary for other sentences of English. What about (4), (6) and (8)? The transformation deleting indefinite elements like *anyone* when they are subjects of embedded sentences without finite verbs is a very common one. Sentence (21) is thus convertible into:

(22) It was easy to please Janice.

and the same **indefinite deletion** transformation removes the *anyone* from (10), (11) and (12) to generate (4), (6) and (8).

So, for example:

(4) The messenger was not hard to follow.

comes from the deep structure (16) which contains an indefinite subject *anyone* for the verb *follow* and which has *the messenger* as the object of *follow*. If the native speaker has in childhood internalized a grammar with properties like those I have described he will have some kind of mental representation roughly analogous to (16). So it is hardly surprising that he understands sentence (4) as if the indefinite subject were physically present on the surface and as if *the messenger* were still in the object position after *follow*.

The incorporation of this more abstract level of language, ill-defined as it still is, as a necessary component of any grammar is one of the major contributions of transformational linguistics. As I pointed out earlier, (16) is only a convenient abbreviation for an abstract structure that might be common to all human languages. The speaker of each language then exploits its **lexicon** or vocabulary and its particular set of transformations to generate the appropriate sentences of his language. This description is, of course, far too general and rather glibly covers areas of language about which too little is yet known.

For instance, in a transformational grammar, when the appropriate words are introduced from the lexicon, they are not represented by their final surface forms (and no one knows how lexical items are represented in the speaker or hearer's mind). Even the best grammatical representation is in dispute. One deep structure might become:

(23) Lane denounced our invasion of Laos.

Or alternatively the structure might take on the form of a nominal unit or nominalization. Nominalizations behave like other nouns in serving as part or all of a noun phrase subject, object, appositive, etc. So (23) is a nominalized structure containing almost exactly the same semantic content as (24):

(24) Lane's denunciation of our invasion of Laos . . .

Currently transformational linguists disagree as to how constructions like those in (12) can best be represented in a grammar. Two major hypotheses are presently being discussed. Those who agree with the "generative semantics" hypothesis would argue that underlying *denunciation* is a verb like *denounce*, that underlying *our invasion of Laos* is a construction like that of:

(25) We invaded Laos.

Others, who prefer the "lexicalist" hypothesis, would deny that a verb *denounce* should, in a sound grammar, underlie *denunciation*, regardless of its historical origin.[1] They would claim no priority either for the sentence version (23) or the nominalized version (24), since either could be present in deep structure. So for lexicalists there is no need for nominalization transformations converting "we invaded Laos" into "our invasion of Laos."

The "generative semanticist" maintains that a transformational grammar must be based on meaning, that underlying the sentences of a human language is an abstract level representing almost all the semantic content. Transformations are applied successively to convert this deep semantic level into the final surface form. So "semantic" and "syntactic" rules are treated as basically the same. The difference is that the earlier or "deeper" rules are those commonly regarded as semantic, while the later or "more surface" rules are those considered as syntactic.

Lexicalists, however, maintain a strict separation between syntactic and semantic rules. The lexicalist model of syntax has no abstract semantic level from which surface forms are generated by syntactic rules. Instead the deep structure level is really a set of sentence **structures**, the form of each structure being restricted by a set of deep structure or "base" rules of the kind that specify, for

---

[1] Strictly speaking there are two disputes. First there is the question as to whether the lexicon is the source for all lexical items except for those generated by very general and regular processes, or whether there is a fairly large number of transformations generating lexical forms. This can be labeled as the **lexicalism–transformationalism** question. Secondly there is the dispute over the precise role of meaning in a grammar. The view that surface structures are generated from underlying meaning is known as **generative semantics**, while the view that there is a deep structure independent of meaning, one requiring interpretation by means of semantic interpretation rules, is called **interpretive semantics**.

example, that a sentence must contain a noun phrase, an auxiliary phrase, and a verb phrase, often shown like this:

Sentence → NP   AUX   VP

Transformations convert these deep structures into surface forms. At various stages between deep and surface levels particular rules of semantic interpretation are applicable, such as those identifying the noun phrase *Laurence* as capable of having the same reference as *he* in the first sentence below, but a different reference in the second sentence.

> (26) Although *he* was tired of all the discussion, *Laurence* could not help joining in.
> (27) *He* was tired of all the discussion although *Laurence* could not help joining in.

Evidence relevant to an intelligent choice between the two hypotheses is hard to find. The lexicalists get rid of much of the transformational machinery by enriching the deep structure and the lexicon and relying heavily on semantic interpretation rules. Thus they claim that deletion transformations are unnecessary. The generative semanticist claims however that:

> (28) Philip disliked Philip's having to work late.

underlies

> (29) Philip disliked having to work late.

A transformation known as **Identical NP Deletion** removes the second of two identical noun phrases. The generative semanticist claims that this not only accounts for the native speaker's intuitions about (29) but also makes (29) quite regular since whenever the two NP's are not identical deletion is not permitted.

> (30) Philip disliked Sharon's having to work late.

Thus (29) is first the quite regular (28) which is changed only because the noun phrases happen to have the same reference.

But the lexicalist does not accept such arguments. There is no (28) he would say. When we read or hear (29) we interpret the lack of a subject for *having to work late* as meaning that a previous noun phrase must be interpreted as subject. Since there are many irregularities and problems in defining identity of noun phrases, the lexicalist would dispense with such transformations and shift the burden to the semantic interpretation rules. Furthermore, while it might seem attractive to simplify the deep or underlying structure level and capture an obvious semantic relation by deriving

(31) Eric's glimpse of Mount Palomar . . .

from

(32) Eric glimpsed Mount Palomar.

what does one do about parallel constructions like

(33) Eric's vision of angels . . .
(34) Eric's contempt for hypocrisy . . .

Generative semanticists have suggested that there are underlying or "abstract" verbs corresponding perhaps to *vide* and *contemn* which *have* to be nominalized. This may have been a historical fact but it is not a fact now. Formulating a grammar with such "abstract" verbs presents some difficulty since rather complex and perhaps counter-intuitive "rules" have to be formulated for specific lexical items, probably in the form of a feature signifying, for example, "apply the type X nominalization rule."

On the other hand the generative semanticist would argue that simplifying the syntax at the expense of having a huge and incredibly complex set of semantic interpretation rules is ridiculous. We know far more about syntax than semantics at present, so shifting more material into the semantic component only complicates matters. The dispute is obviously more complex than this discussion suggests and this is not the place to expand on it. But the dispute seems to be more about the formal machinery of grammars than anything else. In fact the two apparently different types of grammatical machinery may actually be expressing the same kinds of insights about the same range of data. In other words they may be paraphrases differing mainly in terminology. Until more evidence is uncovered, it seems best to reserve judgment while taking advantage of the insights discovered as new grammars are worked out.[2]

---

[2]Indeed it has been shown that all extant versions of transformational grammars (and, of course, any other kind of grammar) are still formally inadequate.

In any case, it is hardly surprising that there are now competing hypotheses in transformational linguistics. The staggering quantity of new research stimulated by Chomsky's earlier work has brought up linguistic phenomena that even the model of grammar presented in Chomsky's *Aspects of the Theory of Syntax* cannot account for. The earlier dispute between the transformational linguists and the old school of structural linguistics was quite different because the transformationalists then concentrated on syntax while the structuralists produced their work primarily in phonology. Today the two groups of transformational linguists are working on the same languages in the same areas—syntax and semantics. Consequently we should be able to compare one with the other while profiting from the insights of both. The present controversy is one natural outcome of the intensity and quantity of fine research that Chomsky's *Syntactic Structures* (1957) first stimulated.

Select Bibliography

General

CHOMSKY, N. *Aspects of the Theory of Syntax*. Cambridge, Mass. : M. I. T. Press, 1965.

JACOBS, R. A. *On Transformational Grammar*. Monograph Series 11, New York State English Council, 1968.

JACOBS, R. A. and ROSENBAUM, P. S. *English Transformational Grammar*. Lexington, Mass. : Xerox College Publishing, 1968.

——. *Readings in English Transformational Grammar*. Lexington, Mass. : Xerox College Publishing, 1970.

——. *Transformations, Style, and Meaning*. Lexington, Mass. : Xerox College Publishing, 1971.

PETERS, S. and RITCHIE, R. W. "On the Generative Power of Transformational Grammars," *Information Sciences* (forthcoming).

---

to account for natural languages. Transformational rules are too powerful since they can generate many combinations that, to the best of our knowledge, never occur in natural language and would not be expected to occur. Consequently the most promising approaches would seem to be those that place severe restrictions on the kinds of transformations allowable. If more narrowly restricted transformations can still account for properties presently accounted for by less restricted ones, then clearly the narrower ones are superior since they will exclude more possibilities that never happen to occur in natural language. The most interesting research in this area is that of Peters and Ritchie (forthcoming).

Generative Semantics

KIPARSKY, PAUL and KIPARSKY, CAROL. "Fact" in Bierwisch and Heidolph (eds.), *Progress in Linguistics*. The Hague: Mouton and Co., 1970.

LAKOFF, G. *Generative Semantics*. New York: Holt, Rinehart & Winston, 1972.

McCAWLEY, J. A. "Where Do Noun Phrases Come From?" in Jacobs and Rosenbaum, *Readings*, 1970.

ROSS, J. R. "On Declarative Sentences" in Jacobs and Rosenbaum, *Readings*, 1970.

Lexicalism

CHOMSKY, N. "Remarks on Nominalization" in Jacobs and Rosenbaum, *Readings*, 1970.

JACKENDOFF, R. S. *Some Rules of Semantic Interpretation for English*. Ph. D. Thesis, M. I. T., 1969.

Two Arguments[1]

This article will present two arguments relevant to the current controversy concerning the role of meaning in a grammar. I have based the arguments on two very fine articles that have appeared recently, one by J. A. Fodor, "Three Reasons for Not Deriving 'Kill' from 'Cause to Die'" in the October, 1970, issue of *Linguistic Inquiry*. This article argues against a major claim of generative semanticists. The other, by Frederick J. Newmeyer, is "On the Alleged Boundary between Syntax and Semantics." This appeared in the May, 1970, issue of *Foundations of Language*. It must be understood that I have taken considerable liberties with their arguments and consequently must accept responsibility for their form in this article.

There has been considerable argument over the way meaning is to be represented in a grammar. The generative semanticists have argued that there is no deep structure level which is distinct from the semantic structure. Consequently, in their deep structures they have had to represent complex meanings even when they are represented at the surface structure level by a single verb. The sentence

(1) Joseph married Catherine last week.

---

[1]This is based on a talk given to a group of English teachers who had already done some work with transformational grammar. They had asked for introductory instruction in following linguistic arguments of the sort that appeared in journals. I have not attempted to summarize the full subject-matter of the articles upon which these remarks are based and have certainly oversimplified.

is, in fact, ambiguous. The less obvious interpretation is that Joseph—a priest, minister, rabbi or town clerk—performed a marriage ceremony, causing Catherine to be linked in matrimony with some unnamed person. Thus underlying (1) is something like the following:

(2) Joseph caused Catherine to be married to *X* last week.

except that (2) is really meant to be a deep structure and a deep structure is, in this case, really a grouping of meanings, some of which come later to be words; others, like **cause**, are really abstract or higher verbs that don't make it to the surface structure, although, of course, the surface structure is understood as if it were there.

Similarly it has been suggested that *kill* be derived from *cause to die* and that the causative meaning of *melt* be derived from a complex underlying construction also containing an abstract **cause** verb. Deriving

(3) Floyd melted the glass.

from an underlying structure

(4) (Floyd **cause** (the glass melt))

provides for the ambiguity of the sentence:

(5) Floyd melted the glass $\left\{\begin{matrix} \text{and that} \\ \text{and it} \\ \text{which} \end{matrix}\right\}$ surprised me.

For many people this last sentence can mean either that I was surprised that Floyd melted the glass, or that I was surprised that the glass melted. That is to say, in the first case the *that*, *it*, or *which* has been substituted for the constituent (*Floyd caused* (*the glass melt*)), while for the other reading they have replaced only **the** subordinated constituent (*the glass melt*). Thus the ambiguity of (5) is strong evidence that the apparently simple sentence

(3) Floyd melted the glass.

is at a deeper level a complex structure containing an embedded sentence. This is evidence that there are transformations which derive words from underlying phrases. These transformations, called lexicalization transformations, are an important part of the generative semantic apparatus.

More ambitiously, lexicalization transformations have been proposed for relating *kill* to *die* by deriving *kill* from something like *cause to die*.

However, it can be argued that there are no such lexicalization transformations or abstract verbs like **cause**. And in fact there are meaning considerations that are not represented by such methods. For example, *kill* is not really synonymous with *cause to die*. This is readily seen when we look, for example, at the behavior of *kill* and *cause to die* in sentences with instrumental adverbial phrases. Of these two sentences only the first is well-formed:

> (6) Albert caused Josephine to die on Sunday by stabbing her on Saturday.
> (7) *Albert killed Josephine on Sunday by stabbing her on Saturday.

All right, you concede, *kill* and *cause to die* are different. But then how does one represent the meaning of *kill*, since your deep structure is the meaning itself? Lexicalists have no such problem since they can fit the appropriate meanings into the semantic interpretation component without making any grammatical claims. In fact, even the *melt* example is open to the same criticism. Of the next two sentences only the first is well-formed:

> (8) Floyd caused the glass to melt on Sunday by heating it on Saturday.
> (9) *Floyd melted the glass on Sunday by heating it on Saturday.

You can **cause** an event by doing something at a time distinct from the time of the event. But if you melt something, then you melt it when it melts.

There are other arguments too, but they are too complex for detailed discussion at this point. Essentially they are based upon the fact that certain major transformations can be applied to the first member of each pair of sentences but not to the second. One such transformation is the "do so" rule, which replaces a verb with *do so* under certain circumstances. Thus the *did so* in (10) really stands for *died*:

> (10) Albert caused Josephina to die and it didn't surprise me that she did so.

On the other hand, this transformation fails with *kill*:

(11) *Albert killed Josephina and it didn't surprise me that she did so.

One possible solution to this problem is to claim that the "do so" transformation applies late in the grammar, after the transformation collapsing *cause to die* into *kill*. Since *do so* is only inserted when the two verbs are identical, it cannot be inserted when the verbs are *kill* and *die*. So this problem is solved.

Or is it? Unfortunately it doesn't work for the two verbs *melt*. There are two perfectly good sentences:

(12) Floyd melted the glass though it surprised me that it would do so.

(13) Floyd melted the glass though it surprised me that he would do so.

In (12) the *do so* has been substituted for the subordinated verb phrase *melt*, while in (13) it has been substituted for the deep structure *cause . . . to melt*. However, to produce (12) the "do so" transformation must have to apply before the transformation collapsing *cause . . . to melt* into *melt*, while to produce (13) the same transformation must have to apply after. Both orderings cannot be correct.

In short, single words like *kill* do not behave like phrases such as *cause to die*. Even where a word and a phrase are synonymous we should expect the phrase to show degrees of syntactic freedom unavailable to single words. With a phrase containing two verbs we can use two time modifiers, say *on Saturday* and *on Sunday*, because there are two verbs capable of receiving them. But when there is only one verb, even if it "means" two verbs, there cannot be two such time modifiers. So, of course, one can say, if awkwardly,

(14) On Saturday I caused Maria to be married on Sunday.

but not

(15) *On Saturday I married Maria on Sunday.

Consequently it seems that *form* rather than *meaning* is the crucial factor here. Attempts to base syntax upon meaning must founder on such a rock. True, it is possible to invent just for this purpose special conditions on the application of the lexicalization rule. But a grammar full of such special conditions is hardly likely to be an optimal one for accounting for the native speaker's intuitions.

Now let's look at a different argument. The verbs *begin* and *start* both imply as part of their meaning that what is begun or started is an activity that *continues* over some period of time, however short. The following sentences each offer a number of interesting meaning possibilities:

(16) The man began dinner.
(17) The man began the book.
(18) The man started the sermon.

Sentence (16) may mean, for example, that the man began *eating* or *cooking* dinner, but not that he began *smelling* it or *enjoying* it. The latter pair of verbs, notice, are verbs to do with *perception*. Similarly (17) allows *reading, writing, translating,* or even, if his taste turned that way, *eating* the book, but not *appreciating, understanding, fearing, being amused at* it, or *being annoyed at* it. This last group of verbs is again made up of verbs of perception. And (18) may mean *writing, composing, delivering,* or *reading,* not *listening to* it even though most of us frequently have to *listen to* them.

Since the lexicalist allows no abstract verbs in the deep structure, he must posit for (16) a deep structure something like this:

(19)

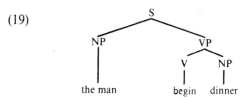

This makes (16) parallel to:

(20) *a* The man ate dinner.
　　b The man read the book.
　　c The man delivered the sermon.

all with a simple subject-verb-object deep structure. Now, according to the lexicalist hypothesis, semantic interpretation rules must provide a semantic interpretation for the sentence. There must, as far as we're concerned here, be two interpretation rules. One must provide that the understood non-perceptual continuing activity is part of the interpretation. We might call this **sense insertion**. The other is that *the man* must be understood as the one doing the understood non-perceptual continuing activity; that is, the subject of the sentence is interpreted as the subject for the "activity," not just the "beginning." This has been called **subject-lowering**. These are both semantic interpretation rules.

Now there is a sentence:

(21) It is likely that the man eats dinner.

which would, according to the lexicalist, have the deep structure:

(22)

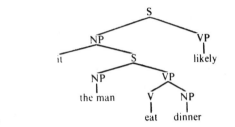

Once the complementizer *that* has been inserted, the extraposition transformation shifts the embedded sentence to the end. Then, once the copula form *is* has been added, we have sentence (21). Alternatively, once *that* has been inserted, we can delete *it* and get

(23) That the man eats dinner is likely.

Note that the deep structure of (21) and (23) requires no **sense-insertion** or **subject-lowering**. It is thus basically the same as the semantic interpretation. But the same deep structure (and semantic interpretation) is valid for:

(24) The man is likely to eat dinner.

Two transformations are necessary to get (24) from the deep structure. (There are others also but they are irrelevant here.) One transformation has been called **"it" replacement** or **subject-raising**. It generates the following intermediate structure:

(25)

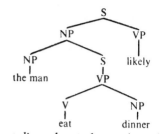

Then the predicate *eat dinner* has to be put into the same verb phrase as *likely*. With the extra NP symbol removed, the result is

(26)

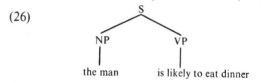

(We have again omitted discussion of other transformations not relevant here.)

So, in the lexicalist framework two transformations are needed: **subject-raising** and **predicate insertion**. And in the interpretative component two semantic rules are needed: **subject-lowering** and **sense-insertion**. Notice that these processes are very similar, but in different parts of the grammar.

The generative semanticist would accept the lexicalist's deep structure for *The man is likely to eat dinner* and also the need for the **subject-raising** and **predicate-insertion** transformations. For him, though, the deep structure *is* the semantic structure. Therefore he uses no **subject-lowering** or **predicate-insertion** rules. But he would also have the same kind of deep structure as (22) for *the man began dinner*. The major difference is that the lower verb is an abstract one:

(27)

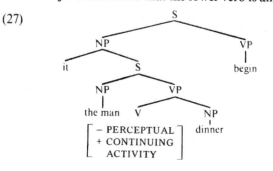

This expresses all the semantic relations relevant here. The syntactic transformations **subject-raising** and **predicate-insertion** generate the right surface structures. And no **subject-lowering** or **sense-insertion** rules are needed. Consequently the generative semanticist can claim that his grammar is a simpler one, without unnecessary and poorly understood semantic rules. In this case a semantically based grammar, using two rules acknowledged to be necessary by lexicalists, can account for phenomena for which lexicalists need an additional quite complex component. Moreover such a grammar is able to relate insightfully sentences which would have to be treated separately in a grammar not based on meaning.

In fact, the *begin* and *likely* verb phrases discussed earlier have other interesting properties:

(28) *a* The man began dinner at noon and the girl began at six.
     b The man is likely to eat dinner at noon and the girl is likely to at six.
     c The man ate dinner at noon and the girl ate at six.

The *c* sentence is interpreted in a different way than *a* or *b* is. In *c* there is no implication in the second half that the girl ate *dinner* at six. It might have been supper, an apple, or anything else that can occur as the object of *eat*. This is easily explained if *eat* in the deep structure can take an indefinite noun phrase *something*. But the girl in *b* can only be understood to be likely to eat dinner. The verb phrase following *likely* can be deleted only if it is identical to the previous verb phrase *eat dinner*. Thus (28)*b* must have undergone **identical verb phrase deletion**. This explains why the sentence allows only the *dinner* interpretation.

The interpretation allowable for (28)*a* is more like that of (28)*b* than *c*. The girl must have begun dinner, not a book, sermon, apple, or siesta. And the missing abstract verb must have the same meaning. So if the man began *eating* dinner, then the girl must also have begun *eating* it, not cooking it. If the man began *cooking* dinner, then so must the girl. This can be accounted for if we assume **identical verb phrase deletion**, as we did before. But this, of course, means that the deep structure must have contained identical abstract verbs, both meaning *cook* or both meaning *eat*, etc. The evidence for such abstract verbs and the semantically based deep structure which they imply demands that we scrutinize very closely other analyses in which deep structures are markedly different from semantic representation. After doing so, one will find numerous other cases suggesting that a non-semantic deep structure can be dispensed with.

Phonology

Features, Classes, and Phonological Generalizations

We are going to look here at some of the English consonants from the viewpoint of the dimensions generative-transformational linguists use in describing them.

Think of a baby uttering its earliest non-crying sounds. Some of them are just vowels, perhaps an "aaah" or that sound rather like the vowel in the "er" we may produce while fumbling for a word. This sound, transcribed as ə "schwa," is produced when the tongue is more or less in a rest position, neither high nor low in the mouth. It is hard to imagine many babies beginning naturally with an i sound like the vowel in *seen*, which requires the tongue to be *high* in the mouth. Similarly an o, as in *boat*,[1] where the tongue is *low* and humped back, is also an unlikely first vowel.[2]

What about the consonants? The first ones are likely to be those produced in the most forward or **anterior** section of the mouth. We might call these the anterior consonants. They include the so-

---

[1]For ease of exposition I ignore in this paper offglides like the |w| in *boat* [bowt]. Customarily phonetic symbols are enclosed in square brackets, and phonemic symbols, that is those standing for linguistically significant units at the phonemic level postulated by structural linguists, are usually shown with slashes. Generative phonologists deny the existence of such a level but use units known as "systematic phonemes," the functions of which are somewhat different. There will be some discussion of this later. In the present group of articles I shall make no distinctions of this nature since these articles are intended as a simple introduction.

[2]See, for example, Roman Jakobson, *Kindersprache, Aphasie, und allgemeine Lautgesetze*. Uppsala: Almqvist and Wiksell, 1941. He claims that [a] or a sound close to it is likely to be the first vowel.

called **labials**, p̲, b̲, m̲, f̲, and v̲, produced when the outgoing air-stream is either cut off or hindered by the coming together of the lips or of the upper lip and lower teeth. They also include the **dentals**, t̲, d̲, n̲, l̲, θ̲ (as in *thin*), ð̲ (as in *this*), s̲ and z̲, produced by the contact of the tongue blade (or **coronal** section) with either the upper teeth or (especially in babies) with the alveolar ridge behind them. Try saying each sound and noticing what happens in the mouth.

If we call these consonants **anterior** consonants, then we might call consonants not made in the anterior of the mouth **non-anterior** consonants. The alveopalatal consonants, č as in *chunk*, ǰ as in *junk*, š as in *pressure*, and ž as in *pleasure*, are made when the blade of the tongue comes into contact with the front part of the hard palate or the back part of the alveolar area. And k̲, g (as in *good*), and ŋ (as in *swing*) are made when the body (not the blade) of the tongue meets the roof of the mouth. Try out each of the non-anterior consonants:

č ǰ š ž̲ k̲ g̲ ŋ

All of these consonants are distinctive in English. That is, substituting one of them for another can change the meaning of a word. Each consonant differs from any other in at least one property, a property or feature which is linguistically distinctive. As an example of a linguistically *non-distinctive* difference we might take the one between the k̲ in *cool*, in which the contact is fairly far back, and the k̲ in *keel*, in which the tongue contact is almost in the palatal position for č as in *choke*. Check this for yourself by saying *cool, keel, cool, keel*. In English the difference between l̲ and r̲ is linguistically significant. In some languages, for example Japanese, the difference is not linguistically distinctive. Hence all the jokes about flied lice.

The linguist is primarily concerned with sounds that are linguistically significant, and the various rules governing their occurrence and modification in specific linguistic environments. He may look at the linguistically significant sounds as units, calling them **phonemes**. The phonemes of a particular language contrast with each other in that language. Corresponding to each phoneme there is at the purely phonetic level a variety of sounds differing from each other only in linguistically non-distinctive ways, like the two k̲'s described above. Such sounds "within" the phoneme[3] have been called **allophones**. Substituting one allophone for another in the same phoneme may make a particular word sound strange, but it will not change the meaning.

Another very productive way to look at speech sounds is to look at the linguistically significant differences between them. Sounds are thus viewed as discrete segments each of which is made up of a bundle of characteristics or features that are distinctive in the language being investigated. Such features are useful for describing natural classes of sounds, groups of sounds that undergo the same phonological processes. The features postulated are ideally the minimum number necessary to represent the significant differences among the sounds. They are furthermore expected by most linguists to have some phonetic basis—acoustic, articulatory, or perceptual. Since in most cases the property or feature is either present or absent, a binary system with plus or minus values has been found to work very well.

The consonants p̲, b̲, θ̲, ð̲, f̲, v̲, t̲, d̲, s̲, and z̲ all involve the anterior part of the mouth, unlike š̲, ž̲, č̲, ǰ, k̲, and g̲. Using the articulatory property of being anterior or non-anterior, we can call the first group of consonants [+ anterior] and the rest [− anterior].

Now suppose that some language just has these consonants and no others:

   p̲ t̲ š̲ ž̲ č̲ ǰ k̲ g̲

Suppose that when p̲ or t̲ begins a word, it is pronounced with a strong puff of air (or **aspirated**). So the p̲ in *pit* will be aspirated while the t̲ is not. Aspiration is shown with a raised *h*. So *pit* is pronounced

---

[3]On the whole, the older school of structural linguists considered these phonemes as constituents of a single phonemic level at which all linguistically significant differences had to be represented. Subsequent work has shown such a level to be an unnecessary and at times misleading complication. See, for example, the first chapter of M. Halle, *The Sound Pattern of Russian* (1959), P. Postal, *Aspects of Phonological Theory* (1968), and my own paper, *Remarks on the Phoneme 1862–1962* (1970). But the notion of the phoneme itself, representing surface contrasts, is a valuable one for both synchronic and diachronic investigation.

p^hit

and *tip* is pronounced

t^hip

In fact, a similar phenomenon actually occurs in English, though the rules are more complex. Compare the two *p*'s in *pit* and *spit* for example.

But back to our imaginary language, which is much simpler. The feature or property that characterizes all and only the consonants that can be [+ aspiration] is their anteriorness. Being [− anterior] thus also means being [− aspiration]. We'll use the letter C as an abbreviation for consonant and write the rule thus:

C
[+ anterior] → [+ aspiration] in word-initial position

That is, anterior consonants are aspirated when they begin a word. This is a simple and general rule abstracting the feature common to just those consonants undergoing aspiration. The features [+ anterior] and [− anterior] thus represent natural classes of sounds within the language, sounds that undergo the same process.

Now let's change the consonant system of the language. The consonants are now

p̱ ḇ ṯ ḏ ḵ g̱

and

s̱ ẕ

The difference between the six consonants of the first group and the two of the second is a matter of duration or continuance. The consonants s̱ and ẕ can be prolonged as long as your breath lasts:

s−s−s−s   z−z−z−z

and they can remain a single sound unit. In this respect they are like vowels. So we'll use the feature **continuance** and say that they are [+ continuant]. The rest occur when the breath is released suddenly in a kind of explosion. Sometimes they are called **stops** or **plosives**. Since they cannot be continued indefinitely as single sounds we'll say they are [− continuant].

Look now just at the [−continuant] consonants. Suppose some rule applied to t̪ and d̪ but not to p, b̪, k̪, or g. Clearly the anterior feature cannot be the determining factor since there are four [+anterior] consonants and only two of them undergo the rule. In what way do p, b̪, k̪, and g differ as a class from t̪ and d̪? The coronal area of the tongue is used only for t̪ and d̪. The others either make use of another part of the tongue or do not involve the tongue at all. So we can classify t̪ and d̪ as [+coronal] (as are also s̪, z̪, š, ž, č, and ǰ in English), and p, b̪, k̪, g as [−coronal]. The satisfactoriness of **coronal** as a feature depends on how natural a class it defines. If many rules affect just those consonants which are coronal, then the feature is justified. In English, as in many other languages, this feature appears well-justified.

To progress to one feature that is especially important in English: here again is our list of [−continuant][4] consonants:

p̪ b̪ t̪ d̪ k̪ g̪

Imagine a rule applying to b̪, d̪, and g but not to p, t̪, and k̪. What should we notice about the two classes? Say aloud p b̪.

The p is a stoppage of the breath stream followed by a little explosion of breath. But it lacks the "buzzing" sound produced by the vibration of the vocal bands down in the larynx. The b̪ has some buzzing or voice associated with it. Here are some voiceless consonants. Pronounce them:

p̪ t̪ f̪ k̪ s̪

Now here are their voiced counterparts:

b̪ d̪ v̪ g̪ z̪

We can label the voiceless class of sounds [−voice] and the others [+voice]. In English all vowels are [+voice] of course.

In English there is an "s" suffix with a number of quite different functions. It serves as a possessive, as a plural ending on nouns, and as a singular ending on present tense verbs in the third person:

---

[4]In fact, the continuance feature is primarily an articulatory rather acoustic feature— whether or not there is a stoppage in the mouth. Under this criterion the nasal consonants m̪, n̪ and ŋ̪ have to be considered [−continuant] since stoppage does occur in the mouth.

(1)*a*   the coat's collar
   b   The coats are over there.
   c   This process coats the ball-bearings with rustproof shellac.

Of course this suffix should probably be considered as three distinct suffixes on the syntactic level. Sometimes it is pronounced s̠, a [− voice] sound. Sometimes it is pronounced z̠, a [+ voice] sound. What rule do native speakers of English follow, unconsciously, when the suffix is used? Listen for yourself. Pronounce each of the following words with the "s" suffix:

(2) *a*   hip   rate   safe   pick
   b   fib   raid   save   pig

When the last *sound* segment (not orthographic symbol) of a word is a [− voice] [− continuant] consonant like p̠, t̠, f̠, or k̠ then the suffix is the [− voice] s̠. But when the word ends in a [+ voice] [− continuant] consonant like b̠, d̠, v̠, and g̠, then the suffix is the [+ voice] one, z̠.

So, treating s̠ as the basic form, we can write a rule like this:

$$\text{s̠} \rightarrow [+ \text{voice}] \text{ after } \begin{bmatrix} + \text{consonant} \\ - \text{continuant} \\ + \text{voice} \end{bmatrix}$$

i.e. a voiceless s̠ becomes voiced after a voiced consonant.

This is, of course, only a very crude approximation of the actual English rule, useful for our purposes. There are related phenomena such as the extra vowel when the suffix is added on to words ending in s̠, z̠, š̠, ž̠, č̠, and ǰ. This suffix is always pronounced z̠. Say *judges*, *fishes*, *churches*. Since the suffix follows a vowel, which is always [+ voice], the [+ voice] z̠ is predictable. Consider the plural forms of *banana*, *guarantee*, etc. The consonants s̠, z̠, š̠, ž̠, č̠, and ǰ, which normally require a vowel between them and the "s" suffix, are the only English sounds that are not only [+ coronal] but also **strident**, that is they have a special high-pitched quality that shows up prominently on acoustic equipment. We call this latter property [+ strident]. All other sound segments are [− strident]. Let's assume that there is a rule inserting a vowel before the "s" suffix when the suffix is added to a word ending in a sound segment which is both

[+ coronal] and [+ strident]. Once this rule has been carried out, we can get rid of the [+ consonant] and [− continuant] restrictions in

$$\text{s} \rightarrow [+ \text{voice}] \text{ after } \begin{bmatrix} + \text{consonant} \\ - \text{continuant} \\ + \text{voice} \end{bmatrix}$$

and write

$$\text{s} \rightarrow [+ \text{voice}] \text{ after } [+ \text{voice}]$$

which is a more general rule. The "s" suffix is voiced whenever it is added to a voiced sound segment. However it might be better not to assume that the "s" suffix is basically voiceless. We could use the symbol S and say that the S agrees in voicing with the preceding sound segment. This will incidentally make it easier to formulate a rule for the voicing or not of the regular past tense endings for words like *sacked* and *sagged*.

Before writing a more precise rule, here are some conventions of rule-writing that you need to know:

1. The phrase "after X" is usually represented by

$$\text{X}\text{———}$$

and "before X" as

$$\text{———X.}$$

2. The line ——— represents the place where the item on the left of the arrow fits in, and the diagonal slash / means *if*.
When two sounds must have the *same* value for a feature, no matter whether it is + or −, the symbol α "alpha" is used in place of + or −.
3. The beginning or end point of a word is marked with the symbol #.

Now here is the rule stating that if the suffix is at the end of a word, it is [+ voice] if the preceding sound segment is [+ voice], and [− voice] if the preceding segment is [− voice].

$$\text{s} \rightarrow [\alpha \text{ voice}] / [\alpha \text{ voice}] \text{———} \#$$

Let's translate this rule, symbol by symbol, into two literal versions:

s	→	[α voice]	/	[ᾱ voice] ——	#
s-suffix	becomes	[+ voice]	if	s-suffix comes after [+ voice]	and at end of word
s-suffix	becomes	[− voice]	if	s-suffix comes after [− voice]	and at end of word

Take another feature, nasality, which characterizes the consonant sounds m̱, ṉ, and ŋ̱ (as in *swing* [swiŋ]). In English, and even more obviously in Spanish, a [+ nasal] consonant occurring before most consonants is made by the same combination of speech organs as the consonant, except, of course, that by lowering the glottis we allow the sound to resonate not only in the mouth but also the nose. It is thus possible to predict the particular form a nasal will take. Suppose there is a negative prefix iṈ in which N stands for the class of nasal consonants m̱, ṉ, and ŋ̱. Of these, m̱ is pronounced in the anterior portion of the mouth without the use of the coronal area of the tongue. So m̱ is

$$\begin{bmatrix} + \text{ nasal} \\ + \text{ anterior} \\ - \text{ coronal} \end{bmatrix}$$

But ṉ, though also nasal and anterior, is pronounced with the coronal area of the tongue. So ṉ is

$$\begin{bmatrix} + \text{ nasal} \\ + \text{ anterior} \\ + \text{ coronal} \end{bmatrix}$$

And ŋ̱, also nasal, is not pronounced in the anterior portion of the mouth and is not pronounced with the coronal area of the tongue. So ŋ̱ is

$$\begin{bmatrix} + \text{ nasal} \\ - \text{ anterior} \\ - \text{ coronal} \end{bmatrix}$$

It happens that p̱, although not a nasal consonant, is an anterior one which is non-coronal, that is p̱ is

$$\begin{bmatrix} + \text{ consonant} \\ - \text{ nasal} \\ + \text{ anterior} \\ - \text{ coronal} \end{bmatrix}$$

In fact it is also like b̰, t̰, d, k̰, and g̰ in being a "stop" or "plosive" consonant, which cannot be prolonged, unlike "continuant" consonants f̰, v̰, s̰, z, š̰, and ž̰. So, using the feature "continuance," we can represent p as

$$
\begin{bmatrix}
+\,\text{consonant} \\
-\,\text{nasal} \\
+\,\text{anterior} \\
-\,\text{coronal} \\
-\,\text{continuant} \\
-\,\text{voice}
\end{bmatrix}
$$

Now look at this set of features for t̰ and be sure you understand what each feature represents:

$$
\begin{bmatrix}
+\,\text{consonant} \\
-\,\text{nasal} \\
+\,\text{anterior} \\
+\,\text{coronal} \\
-\,\text{continuant} \\
-\,\text{voice}
\end{bmatrix}
$$

And then check over those for g̰

$$
\begin{bmatrix}
+\,\text{consonant} \\
-\,\text{nasal} \\
-\,\text{anterior} \\
-\,\text{coronal} \\
-\,\text{continuant} \\
+\,\text{voice}
\end{bmatrix}
$$

The important features to note for the present are the anterior and coronal ones. These features separate the three consonants.

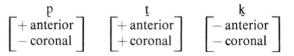

$$
\overset{p}{\begin{bmatrix} +\,\text{anterior} \\ -\,\text{coronal} \end{bmatrix}}
\qquad
\overset{t}{\begin{bmatrix} +\,\text{anterior} \\ +\,\text{coronal} \end{bmatrix}}
\qquad
\overset{k}{\begin{bmatrix} -\,\text{anterior} \\ -\,\text{coronal} \end{bmatrix}}
$$

There are matching features for the nasals:

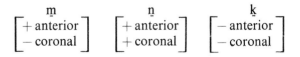

$$
\overset{m}{\begin{bmatrix} +\,\text{anterior} \\ -\,\text{coronal} \end{bmatrix}}
\qquad
\overset{n}{\begin{bmatrix} +\,\text{anterior} \\ +\,\text{coronal} \end{bmatrix}}
\qquad
\overset{k}{\begin{bmatrix} -\,\text{anterior} \\ -\,\text{coronal} \end{bmatrix}}
$$

Here now are three words beginning with p̣, ṭ, or ḳ:

    possible   tangible   capable

We prefix them with the negative prefix iN (where N means nasal)

    iNpossible   iNtangible   iNcapable

An English speaker will intuitively use the particular nasal with the same anterior and coronal features as the consonant following it. Check this out. The spelling does not, of course, necessarily represent the real pronunciation of the nasal.

    impossible   intangible   incapable

English orthography uses no ŋ character. So the symbol n̠ in *incapable* actually stands for the pronunciation ŋ.

In all the examples given, the feature system with its pluses and minuses has been a useful and insightful tool for representing natural classes of sounds within a given language, that is those groups of sounds which undergo particular phonological processes in that language. Sounds, like atoms, are no longer seen as single unshatterable entities but as complexes of the sound features important to a language.

Distinctive Features and Generative Grammar

It was Roman Jakobson who in 1938 suggested a classification of consonants on the basis of linguistically significant acoustic oppositions—or distinctive features as we might call them now.[1] Though such a development had been implicit in the work of Trubetzkoy, Trubetzkoy's writings had treated the phoneme as an indivisible unit. As such there had been no clear way to determine what were common shared elements or features. Jakobson's analysis had two advantages. First, vowels and consonants could be classified using the same kinds of contrasts: voiced and voiceless, rounded and unrounded, tense and lax, etc. The features were intended as a set of universal features, of which each language would use a subset. Thus English, which has no voiced/voiceless contrast in vowels, does have a tense/lax contrast in vowels. The vowel in *loop* is tense [+ tense], while the vowel in *look* is lax [− tense]. The second advantage was that treating phonemes as bundles of binary distinctive features was more economical since there were fewer features than phonemes. Jakobson was able to express linguistically significant contrasts with a minimal number of features. However, Jakobson's attempt to base his features solely on acoustic properties was not successful. His features were defined according to the distribution of energy at different sound-wave frequencies. Unfortunately, all the linguistically-significant likenesses and differences did not

---

[1] R. Jakobson, "Observations sur le classement phonologique des consonnes," *Proceedings of the Third International Congress of Phonetic Sciences 3* (1938) pp. 34–41.

correlate with the spectrographs showing energy distribution. So the feature systems used by generative grammarians today are not restricted to acoustically based features.

What generative grammarians like Chomsky and Halle did was to take over the feature analysis and fit it into a generative-transformational framework. The phonological processes of a language were no longer regarded as independent of higher-level syntactic processes. Indeed syntactic facts were involved in many phonological processes, most notably stress-assignment in English.

We can do no more here than outline in a rather oversimplified manner the structure of a transformational grammar. Until fairly recently it was agreed that any language had a set of quite abstract deep structures, formed according to a limited set of phrase-structure rules. These deep structures embodied the basic grammatical relations essential for semantic interpretation. At this deep level, meaning was derived by means of a set of semantic interpretation rules operating on deep structure sentences. Transformational rules (and some not very clearly specified morphophonemic rules) converted the deep structures into surface structures. At this point the various fairly abstract grammatical elements were replaced by sequences of bundles of features provided in a lexicon or dictionary, one which listed all and only the unpredictable sound-features for each segment of the grammatical elements making up sentences. The predictable features were provided by means of a partially ordered set of interpretative phonological rules such as those which convert the k̲ segment in *specific* to an s̲ segment when the ending -ity follows. Although a number of revisions have been suggested concerning the role of semantics in the grammar, the role of phonology as an interpretative component has not been seriously challenged. However it now seems unlikely that phonological rules can be separated from higher level rules as watertightly as our outline suggests.

The task of a set of distinctive features is to characterize the linguistically significant properties of each sound segment. Sounds more or less alike should have more or less the same features, and the features should represent significant classes or groupings of segments.

The most obvious division among sound segments is between consonants and vowels. Consonants like p̲, b̲, t̲, d̲, č (as in *chair*), j̲ (as in *jeer*), k̲, and g̲ are made by stopping up the outgoing breath for a moment and then releasing it. The stoppage is made with different organs, depending on the consonant produced. Other consonants like θ̱ (as in *thin*), ð̱ (as in *then*), f̱, v̱, s̱, z, š̱ (as in *she*), ẕ̌ (as in *leisure*), ḻ and ṟ, while not involving a stoppage are characterized by a fair degree of obstruction of the breath stream by speech organs. Vowels do not have any such stoppages or obstructions. This property or feature is the **consonantal** feature. Vowels are [− consonantal] while p̱, f̱, g̱, and the other consonants mentioned are [+ consonantal]. The so-called semi-vowels w̱ and y̱, since they involve almost no obstruction, or at least too little to be important here, are [− consonantal]. Some of the consonants: ḻ and ṟ, and the three nasals in English, m̱, ṉ, and ŋ (as in *swing*) are more resonant or **sonorant** than the rest. In this respect they are somewhat vowel-like. The semi-vowels w̱ and y̱ are also sonorant in this respect. So all of these (and the vowels) could be characterized as [+ sonorant] while the other consonants are [− sonorant].

So now the consonants ḻ, ṟ, m̱, ṉ, and ŋ are distinct from the other consonants. Distinctive features must, by definition, distinguish each linguistically significant sound segment. Since m̱, ṉ, and ŋ are all produced with air resonating in the nasal cavity as well as the oral cavity, they are [+ nasal] and in English all other segments are [− nasal].

The semi-vowels y̱ and w̱ are distinct from the vowels in that the latter can by themselves form syllables. (Remember that the y in *dairy* is really an i̱, not a y sound). So vowels are [+ syllabic] and semi-vowels are [− syllabic]. Here now are the features for the different kinds of English sound segments:

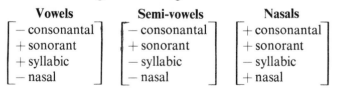

Vowels	**Semi-vowels**	**Nasals**
− consonantal	− consonantal	+ consonantal
+ sonorant	+ sonorant	+ sonorant
+ syllabic	− syllabic	− syllabic
− nasal	− nasal	+ nasal

ḻ, ṟ   The other consonants (call them **Obstruents**)

+ consonantal	+ consonantal
+ sonorant	− sonorant
− syllabic	− syllabic
− nasal	− nasal

So four features differentiate the major groups of sound segments in English. Moreover it can be seen that vowels and semi-vowels, which share three features with identical values, must be expected to be very similar, while vowels and "the other consonants" sharing only one feature, the absence of nasality, are very different. The features for l and r are expectedly not so different from those of "the other consonants" (or obstruents, the name for [− sonorant] consonants). If the nasal feature is regarded (as it should be) as of less importance than the other, more major features, then nasals are less different from vowels than consonants like p, t, and v are. In fact, the syllabic and nasal features of "the other consonants" need not be marked since in English any [+ consonantal] [− sonorant] sound segment must be [− syllabic] and [− nasal]. Similarly any [− consonantal] segment must be [− nasal] in English, though this is not true for some other languages.

How are the members of the major classes described above to be differentiated? Of the main group of consonants, ten are produced in the anterior section of the mouth. Some phonological rules apply only to these [+ anterior] consonants and not to the rest.

[+ anterior]	[− anterior]
p, b, f, v, θ, ð, t, d, s, z	š, ž, č, j, k, g

Both classes contain consonants produced in part by the "coronal area" or "blade" of the tongue. So the last six [+ anterior] consonants and the first four [− anterior] ones are also [+ coronal]. The others are [− coronal]. Next some consonants can be prolonged or continued, like θ, f, s, etc. while others cannot. Since this difference is important to many phonological rules, it requires a feature to represent it. So the continuable segments are [+ continuant] and the remainder [− continuant].[2] Here is a summary of the anterior, coronal, and continuant values for the [− nasal] consonants:

	p	b	f	v	θ	ð	t	d	s	z	š	ž	č	j	k	g
Anterior	+	+	+	+	+	+	+	+	+	+	−	−	−	−	−	−
Coronal	−	−	−	−	+	+	+	+	+	+	+	+	+	+	−	−
Continuant	−	−	+	+	+	+	−	−	+	+	+	+	−	−	−	−

---

[2]Actually the continuance feature is relevant only for the oral vowels. The more technical definition refers to the presence or absence of oral stoppage. Since the oral speech organs are in the same positions for the nasals as they are for obstruent [− continuant] segments, the nasals are considered to be [− continuant].

From the table above you should be able to see that the following share the same values for all three features:

(1) p̱, ḇ   (5) ṣ, ẓ
(2) f̱, ṿ   (6) š̱, ẕ̌
(3) θ̱, ð̱   (7) č̱, j̱
(4) ṯ, ḏ   (8) ḵ, g̱

In fact the third pair has the same features as the fifth. However p is significantly different from ḇ in English, and f̱ from ṿ, θ̱ from ð̱, etc. Our present features do not show this. When the second member of each pair is pronounced, there is a buzzing or voicing that is absent from the first member. Pronounce each pair and see. The voicing feature is thus the critical one. The first member of each pair is voiceless or [− voice] and the second [+ voice]. So now ṯ and ḏ, for example, have different feature segments:

$$
\begin{matrix}
t \\
\begin{bmatrix}
+ \text{anterior} \\
+ \text{coronal} \\
- \text{continuant} \\
- \text{voice}
\end{bmatrix}
\end{matrix}
\qquad
\begin{matrix}
d \\
\begin{bmatrix}
+ \text{anterior} \\
+ \text{coronal} \\
- \text{continuant} \\
+ \text{voice}
\end{bmatrix}
\end{matrix}
$$

There is one further problem. The segments for ṣ and θ̱ are still alike, as are ẓ and ð̱. When ṣ or ẓ are made, the air not only has to squeeze through a very narrow opening, but also it strikes the back of the teeth. The same is true for š̱, ẕ̌, č̱, and j̱. The result is that these segments are noisier, or more **strident**. On the other hand, θ̱ and ð̱ are hardly strident at all. So if we add the stridency feature, these segments are differentiated.

	ṣ	θ̱	ẓ	ð̱
Anterior	+	+	+	+
Coronal	+	+	+	+
Continuant	+	+	+	+
Voice	−	−	+	+
Strident	+	−	+	−

Although š̱, ẕ̌, č̱, and j̱ are also [+ strident], this feature is not so important for them since there are no [− strident] consonants in English which otherwise have the same features.

The stridency feature is important in a number of rules. For example, when the plural suffix appears after a [+ strident] consonant, an additional vowel is inserted between them, as in the plurals of *iris, fez, dish, ditch, ridge.*

The three nasal consonants are differentiated from each other by the anterior and coronal features discussed above:

$$
\overset{\underset{\mathtt{\sim}}{m}}{\begin{bmatrix} + \text{anterior} \\ - \text{coronal} \end{bmatrix}}
\qquad
\overset{\underset{\mathtt{\sim}}{n}}{\begin{bmatrix} + \text{anterior} \\ + \text{coronal} \end{bmatrix}}
\qquad
\overset{\eta}{\begin{bmatrix} - \text{anterior} \\ - \text{coronal} \end{bmatrix}}
$$

There is a nasal sound which is [− anterior] and [+ coronal] but it is not a basic segment of English as it is in Spanish. It can be produced in English however as the result of an ṇ coming into contact with an i̬ under certain conditions. This nasal is the [ñ] of *onion.*

The other [+ consonantal] [+ sonorant] segments ḷ and ṛ, sometimes called liquids, are differentiated by the feature of **lateralness**. When ḷ is made, the center of the tongue from the back to the front is raised so as to stop the air stream flowing over it while the sides are kept low. So the air stream is released along one or both sides. (The word *lateral* comes from the Latin word for "side".) So ḷ is [+ lateral]. But ṛ is usually formed with the tip of the tongue touching the upper teeth or alveolar ridge behind them. There are two major forms of ḷ in English. Compare the ḷ's in *keel* and *bowl.* For most people the tip of the tongue is forward in *keel*, somewhat retracted in *bowl.* But these differences are caused by the vowels next to them; they are not basic to the language. The Diegueño language, an American Indian language of the Yuman family spoken in southern California, has four ḷ sounds, but the differences are linguistically significant in themselves rather than a result of their position in a word. There are various kinds of ṛ in English, but the differences are either dialect differences or the result of their position in a word.

The features used to distinguish among vowels are not, in English, distinctive for consonants. In other languages, however, they may be distinctive. The vowels are all articulated in the non-anterior part of the mouth. But the tongue is in a different position for each of them. For the i̬ sound in *heat*, the mouth is only a little open, the tongue quite high up and the body of the tongue is toward the front of the mouth. Compare the vowel sounds in the following words:

i̬	u̬
heat	hoot

The tongue has to be moved fairly far back in the mouth for the u̠. In order to avoid any confusion with the **anterior** feature, we choose **backness** rather than **frontness** as the feature. So u̠ is [+ back] while i̠ is [− back]. But i̠ differs from the æ in *hat* in tongue **height** rather than backness. Compare the vowels:

i̠	æ
heat	hat

So i̠ is [+ high] and æ is [− high]. If you compare two back vowels, you will find the same kind of height difference in u̠ and ɔ̠ (sometimes called "open o"):

u̠	ɔ̠
hoot	ought

So u̠ is also [+ high] and ɔ̠ is [− high].

But the binary feature system presents us with a problem here. There are *three* main tongue heights. So we cannot just use [+ high] and [− high]. Say

i̠	e̠	æ
beat	bait	bat

and also

u̠	o̠	ɔ̠
coot	coat	caught

Your tongue goes down not only from the i̠ and u̠ but also from the e̠ and o̠. Two features can do the job even though not all the plus and minus combinations are used. The features are used rather after the fashion of the grand old Duke of York (according to one version of a nursery rhyme).

> The grand old Duke of York
> He had ten thousand men.
> He marched them up to the top of the hill
> And he marched them down again.
>
> And when they were up, they were up.
> And when they were down, they were down.
> And when they were only halfway up
> They were neither up nor down.

So if i̱ as in *beat* is [+ high] and [− low], and æ, as in *bat* is [− high] and [+ low], then e̱, as in *bait*, being only half-way up, is neither high nor low. So [− high] and [− low] are the features for the middle position. The same treatment is used for the back vowels:

$$
\overset{\text{u̱}}{\begin{bmatrix} + \text{ back} \\ + \text{ high} \\ - \text{ low} \end{bmatrix}}
\quad
\overset{\text{o̱}}{\begin{bmatrix} + \text{ back} \\ - \text{ high} \\ - \text{ low} \end{bmatrix}}
\quad
\overset{\text{ɔ̱}}{\begin{bmatrix} + \text{ back} \\ - \text{ high} \\ + \text{ low} \end{bmatrix}}
$$

There is another important back vowel, the a̱ in *father* (for most non-Bostonian speakers). It is obviously [+ low] and [+ back]. It differs importantly from the other back vowels in that it requires no lip-rounding. In English the lips are **rounded** when we say the back vowels u̱, o̱, and ɔ̱. They are unrounded for the [− back] vowels, i̱, e̱, and æ. So, like all the front vowels, a̱ is [− round]. One other unrounded back vowel is the "schwa," ə, which is the form vowels take in unstressed position. Compare the second vowel in *photography*, a stressed vowel, with its unstressed version in *photograph* (spoken unpedantically, of course); compare the first i̱ in *fertility* and *fertile*. Like e̱, the ə is neither high nor low. There is also a rather insignificant "barred i" written ɨ, which is the second vowel in *roses* for many speakers of British or American English. This is a high back vowel, also unrounded. (Note that none of the unrounded back vowels has the tongue as far back as the round ones. In more traditional terminology, they are **central** vowels.)

Relative to the tongue position the vowels can be shown thus:

$$
\begin{array}{c|cc|cc}
 & [-\text{ back}] & & [+\text{ back}] & \\
\begin{bmatrix} + \text{ high} \\ - \text{ low} \end{bmatrix} & \text{i̱} & & \text{ɨ} & \text{u̱} \\
\begin{bmatrix} - \text{ high} \\ - \text{ low} \end{bmatrix} & \text{e̱} & & \text{ə} & \text{o̱} \\
\begin{bmatrix} - \text{ high} \\ + \text{ low} \end{bmatrix} & \text{æ} & & \text{a̱} & \text{ɔ̱} \\
 & [-\text{ round}] & & [+\text{ round}] &
\end{array}
$$

These are not the only English vowels, of course. For many vowels there is a **tense/lax** contrast. Compare the i̱ in *seat* with the i̱ in *sit*. Apart from the audible pitch difference, there is a difference in the tenseness of the muscles. The i̱ in *seat* is [+ tense]; the i̱ in *sit* is [− tense] or lax. The same contrast is to be found in the [+ tense] e̱ in *bait* and the [− tense] e̱ in *bet*. (Sometimes the tense forms are written with a macron above them: ī, ē). The [+ tense] u̱ in *boon* contrasts with the [− tense] u̱ in *book*. Of the unrounded vowels both i̱ and ə̱ are [− tense]. The æ is also [− tense]. It has no [+ tense] counterpart. In English, syllables can end either in a vowel or one or more consonants. But [− tense] vowels must always be in syllables ending with one or more consonants, that is, in *closed* rather than *open* syllables.

Here is a summary of the vowel features just discussed. Of course all the vowel segments are (in English) [− consonantal], [+ sonorant], [+ syllabic], [− nasal] and [+ voiced]. Tense vowels are shown with a macron.

	ī	i	ē	ę	æ	i̱	ə	ā	ū	u	ō	ɔ̱
High	+	+	−	−	−	+	−	−	+	+	−	−
Low	−	−	−	−	+	−	−	+	−	−	−	+
Back	−	−	−	−	−	+	+	+	+	+	+	+
Round	−	−	−	−	−	−	−	−	+	+	+	+
Tense	+	−	+	−	−	−	−	+	+	−	+	+

Of the semi-vowels (or **glides**, as they are often called), y differs from w in being [− round] as well as [− back]. The so-called glottal glide h is [− high], [− low], while y and w are both high, that is [+ high], [− low]. However h is more like p and similar consonants in being [− sonorant], and its function under some phonological processes is not unlike theirs.

We have now seen that a relatively small set of features, distinctive features, can be used to characterize the linguistically-significant contrasts in English and, indeed, in any language.

However two facts must be remembered. First these all represent a higher, more abstract level, not the gross acoustic signal we actually are exposed to nor even a close phonetic transcription. The plus and minus values must in many cases be converted through low-level phonetic rules into multigraded values. For example, the [+ tense] i in *obscene* is less tense than the [+ tense] i in the French word *ni* (English *neither*). So the pluses may have to be converted into numeral values, for example 1, 2, 3, 4, referring to the degree of tenseness. The second fact is that linguists may replace some of the features described with new ones which better capture significant facts and generalizations about human languages. Indeed, from the cross-linguistic point of view, the plus and minus at the more abstract levels can be replaced with "m" for *marked* and "u" for *unmarked*. *Marked* means roughly "not what one might expect in most languages" and *unmarked* means "just what one would expect." Thus voicing would be unmarked for vowels in most languages. If a vowel had "m" for voicing, we would know it was unvoiced. This is not the place for a full explanation of the theory of markedness. But such a notation should make it much simpler to make cross-linguistic generalizations about phonological processes as well as to characterize certain types of historical change.

The Vowel Shift and English Orthography

For generations it has been a commonplace to speak of the almost whimsical arbitrariness of the English spelling system. Yet at the same time it has become popular to argue for a "phonic" method of teaching reading. Children must learn to "sound out" the letters, people say. Of course, not so long ago, children were taught to "read" words by the Alphabetic Method "si-ey-ti, *cat*," "ar-yuw-en, *run*," and so on. More recent "linguistic approaches" have dealt mainly with surface regularities, some of which can be learned just as well by "look and say" techniques. Teaching children that the sound a̲y̲n̲ is spelled not only "ine" but also "ign," as in *sign*, is not enou̲g̲h as a "linguistic approach." The spelling with g̲ is not arbitrary. It is a morphophonemic rendering for which the g̲ is quite necessary. The tense vowel a̲y̲ in *sign* loses its tenseness under certain conditions and becomes i̲ as in *sit*. When this happens the underlying g̲ surfaces and we have words like *signature, signal, designated, resignation*, etc. The g̲ in *sign* thus serves as a silent signal for the native-speaker, one that indicates that putting certain endings on *sign* will produce a result quite different from that produced by putting the endings on *sine*. The "illogical" final n̲ in *condemn* becomes quite logical when the suffix *-ation* is added.

Denunciations of the alphabet have too often been based on the unquestioned assumption that an alphabet should be little more than a phonetic rendering of the sounds of our language. As distinguished a grammarian as Otto Jespersen has complained:

> With all its imperfections this alphabet might have been capable of representing the sounds of one particular language with tolerable accuracy, if it had been turned to account systematically by trained phoneticians knowing exactly what sounds to represent and then adapting the existing means to the ends.[1]

Fortunately the trained phoneticians did not get their hands on the spelling system. Had they tried in a systematic way to determine "exactly what sounds" had to be represented, they might not have found it easy to determine which sounds from which of the dialects of English merited representation. After all, separate spelling systems, even for the major dialect divisions, would be ruinously expensive, apart from the other major drawbacks of such a scheme.

It is not really so nonsensical to use the letter *c* to stand for both the ḳ and the ṣ sound, or the letter *t* to stand for both ṭ and ṣ̌ (sh). The use of *c* for the final ḳ sound in *electric* is a signal to apply a particular phonological process, one that native speakers use, when endings like *-ian* or *-ity* but not *-al* are applied. A similar relationship is represented by *t* in *transit* and *transition*.

In this paper I shall draw from the recent work of Chomsky and Halle[2] to demonstrate a group of phonological processes which are significant in the ways they affect the quality of the underlying vowels represented in the English spelling system. I shall refer especially to the Vowel Shift Rule, a synchronic rule that came into being as a result of the historical process known as the Great Vowel Shift. (The term synchronic refers to the study of the language as it is at a particular point in time, rather than as it develops across time or diachronically.)

Note the sound of the second vowel in the following list:

    serenity
    convention
    obscenity
    displeasure
    supremacy

---

[1] Otto Jespersen, *A Modern English Grammar on Historical Principles*, Part One (London: George Allen and Unwin, 1961), pp. 1–2.

[2] Chomsky, Noam, and Halle, Morris, *The Sound Pattern of English* (New York: Harper and Row, 1968).

The second vowel, ẹ, is neither a high vowel nor a low one. It differs significantly from ọ, which is also [− high] and [− low] in that it is not produced toward the back of the mouth; that is, it is [− back], whereas ọ is [+ back]. It is a stressed vowel, [+ stress] unlike the first vowel of "serenity." Because the first vowel is unstressed it has been reduced to the neutral vowel ə ("schwa") by a very common process known as **Vowel Reduction**. Stressed vowels cannot be so reduced. Finally this ẹ is not tense in the way that the ẹ sound in *feign* is tense. The muscles are much looser. So our ẹ can be represented thus (using V for "vowel" as an abbreviation for major features differentiating vowels from other groups of sounds):

$$
\begin{matrix} \mathbf{V} \\ \begin{bmatrix} -\text{ high} \\ -\text{ low} \\ -\text{ back} \\ +\text{ stress} \\ -\text{ tense} \end{bmatrix} \end{matrix}
$$

Now for each of the words in the list above there is a corresponding form in which the second vowel, though still spelled with an *e*, is pronounced with a tense [+ tense] īy sound like the vowel in *beat*. (The macron (ˉ) represents tenseness). In this case the vowel is the final vowel of each word. Here are the pairs:

ẹ	īy
serenity	serene
convention	convene
obscenity	obscene
displeasure	displease
supremacy	supreme

The alternation of a single vowel sound ẹ with a diphthong containing the glide y is not important here. English, unlike French or Italian, always diphthongizes its tense vowels. Non-back vowels take the front glide y, while back vowels have the back glide w, like the ūw in "two" or the ōw in *boat*. The process is known as **Diphthongization**.

Historically the second vowel in *serene* was once a tense ē, which was diphthongized to ēy, rhyming with *feign* or the last vowel in "obey." Then, as a result of a sound change known as the **Great**

Vowel Shift, various groupings of vowels changed places. The $\bar{e}$ in $\underline{\bar{e}y}$ became $\bar{\imath}$. Thus, before the Great Vowel Shift (which was actually a long and sometimes gradual process), the second vowel in all the words in the two columns above was not only spelled *e* but pronounced e, except that it became non-tense [− tense] under certain conditions, for example when it was not the last vowel in the word.[3] We might call this process **Laxing.** Otherwise the tense $\bar{e}$ was diphthongized:

$$\bar{e} \rightarrow \underline{\bar{e}y}$$

Then the Great Vowel Shift added a new process if the vowel was stressed (we mark stress with ´):

$$\acute{\bar{e}}y \rightarrow \acute{\bar{\imath}}y$$

Synchronically a like process has to be postulated if we are to account for the sound alternations described above. The underlying representation of the word *serene* does not need the third *e*, which is simply a device for representing tenseness. So we shall assume that after the stress has been assigned (by regular rules that we cannot describe here), we have the underlying form:

$$\underline{ser\acute{e}n}$$

Then the following processes apply:

$\underline{ser\acute{e}n} \rightarrow \underline{ser\acute{e}yn}$	by Diphthongization
$\underline{ser\acute{e}yn} \rightarrow \underline{ser\acute{\imath}yn}$	by Vowel Shift

which the Vowel Reduction Rule converts into the current pronunciation $\underline{sər\acute{\imath}yn}$. The change from $\acute{\bar{e}}$ to $\acute{\underline{\imath}}$ is easily represented by a rule using features:

---

[3]Note that in this paper we are considerably oversimplifying the actual processes in English, which involve a more complex interaction of more precise rules and environments than we can present here. Both the rules and the environments have been narrowed down here to facilitate understanding by the novice in phonology. For more elaborate and complete treatments, see for example, Chomsky, N. and Halle, M. *The Sound Pattern of English*, especially pp. 171–223, and P. Wolfe, *The Great Vowel Shift* (forthcoming).

$$\begin{bmatrix} V \\ -\text{high} \\ -\text{low} \\ +\text{stress} \\ +\text{tense} \\ -\text{back} \end{bmatrix} \rightarrow \begin{bmatrix} V \\ +\text{high} \\ -\text{low} \\ +\text{stress} \\ +\text{tense} \\ -\text{back} \end{bmatrix}$$

that is, the feature [−high] becomes [+high]. This can be shown differently if we wish to separate the crucial features [high] and [low] from the others. We can say that a stressed, tense non-back vowel becomes high if it happens to be both non-high and non-low. The horizontal line inside the last pair of brackets indicates that the environment for the change is present *among* the features of the vowel to be changed.

$$\begin{bmatrix} V \\ +\text{stress} \\ +\text{tense} \\ -\text{back} \end{bmatrix} \rightarrow [+\text{high}] \Bigg/ \begin{bmatrix} \overline{} \\ -\text{high} \\ -\text{low} \end{bmatrix}$$

However when the underlying form <u>serén</u> has the noun suffix <u>iti</u> (spelled -*ity*):

<u>serén</u> + <u>iti</u>

the é, no longer the final vowel, does not undergo Diphthongization and Vowel Shift. Instead the Laxing Rule applies. This makes tense vowels non-tensed before a consonant plus any of the suffixes -*ic*, -*id*, -*ish*, -*ity*, -*ify*, as well as before certain other combinations. So the tenseness changes:

$$\begin{bmatrix} V \\ -\text{high} \\ -\text{low} \\ +\text{stress} \\ +\text{tense} \\ -\text{back} \end{bmatrix} \rightarrow \begin{bmatrix} V \\ -\text{high} \\ -\text{low} \\ +\text{stress} \\ -\text{tense} \\ -\text{back} \end{bmatrix}$$

The segment on the right is a non-tense (or "lax") ę. The resulting form <u>serén</u> + <u>iti</u> becomes <u>sərén</u> + <u>iti</u> by the usual vowel reduction process.

Here now is a different underlying form:

<u>divín</u>

which might have ended up rhyming with *bean*, were it not also subject to Vowel Shift, etc. It becomes

<u>divíyn</u>   (by Diphthongization)

The Vowel Shift has to apply a little differently this time. In our first example the [− high] feature became [+ high]. The stressed tense vowel in <u>divíyn</u> is already [+ high]. So the Vowel Shift changes it the other way:

[+ high] → [− high]

This can be expressed more elaborately in two ways:
either

$$
\begin{matrix} \mathbf{V} \\ \begin{bmatrix} + \text{high} \\ - \text{low} \\ + \text{stress} \\ + \text{tense} \\ - \text{back} \end{bmatrix} \end{matrix} \rightarrow \begin{matrix} \mathbf{V} \\ \begin{bmatrix} - \text{high} \\ - \text{low} \\ + \text{stress} \\ + \text{tense} \\ - \text{back} \end{bmatrix} \end{matrix}
$$

or equivalently

$$
\begin{matrix} \mathbf{V} \\ \begin{bmatrix} + \text{stress} \\ + \text{tense} \\ - \text{back} \end{bmatrix} \end{matrix} \rightarrow [- \text{high}] \Big/ \begin{bmatrix} + \text{high} \\ - \text{low} \end{bmatrix}
$$

In any case, after the vowel shift, <u>divíyn</u> has become <u>divéyn</u> (which actually was one older pronunciation, sounding like the modern word *de-vein*).

So far the Vowel Shift has been described as two processes both of which change the value of the feature [high]. One converts [− high] to [+ high], as in <u>seríyn</u>, the other [+ high] to [− high], as in <u>divéyn</u>. These can be shown as really a single process affecting the values for the [high] feature. If we use the symbol α to mean "either plus or minus," then we can assume that a change from α to − α is a change from one value (either plus or minus) to its opposite. So we can write that a stressed, tense, non-back vowel becomes the opposite in height to what it is already, that is

$$
\begin{bmatrix} V \\ + \text{ stress} \\ + \text{ tense} \\ - \text{ back} \end{bmatrix} \rightarrow [-\alpha\,\text{high}] \Bigg/ \begin{bmatrix} \underline{\qquad} \\ \alpha\,\text{high} \\ - \text{ low} \end{bmatrix}
$$

1   2   3   4   5

To make sure this is clear I have numbered the items in the Vowel Shift above and here append a further explanation:

1. A vowel which is stressed, tense, and non-back
2. becomes
3. one with a certain value for [high]
4. if
5. it is the opposite value for [high] to begin with and it is also non-low.

This switching of the values for the [high] feature is known as the first part of the Vowel Shift Rule. It affects only the non-low vowels i̇́ and ế, raising ế to i̇́ or lowering i̇́ to ế.

There is also an important second part. See if you can interpret this representation of it:

Vowel Shift Part II

$$
\begin{bmatrix} V \\ + \text{ stress} \\ + \text{ tense} \\ - \text{ back} \end{bmatrix} \rightarrow [-\alpha\,\text{low}] \Bigg/ \begin{bmatrix} \underline{\qquad} \\ \alpha\,\text{low} \\ - \text{ high} \end{bmatrix}
$$

1   2   3   4   5

This second part changes [+low] to [−low] for stressed, tense, non-back vowels. The vowel fitting this description is ǽ as in *hat*. Here are the relevant features:

$$
\begin{bmatrix} V \\ + \text{ low} \\ - \text{ high} \\ + \text{ stress} \\ + \text{ tense} \\ - \text{ back} \end{bmatrix}
$$

The second part of the Vowel Shift converts it into a segment with the opposite value for [low], that is .

$$\begin{bmatrix} \text{V} \\ -\text{low} \\ -\text{high} \\ +\text{stress} \\ +\text{tense} \\ -\text{back} \end{bmatrix}$$

which is é̞. Once the usual Diphthongization Rule has added the glide y, the result is é̞y, rhyming with *sleigh* and *grey*. However, as in the case discussed earlier, if the vowel is not final but is followed by a consonant plus one of the endings *-ic*, *-id*, *-ish*, *-ity*, *-ify*, as well as some other combinations, the Laxing Rule makes the stressed vowel non-tense. Thus Diphthongization and Vowel Shift cannot apply.

If we start with the form

insǽn + iti

it then becomes

insǽn + iti   (by the Laxing Rule).

which is spelled out as "insanity" and rhymes with "vanity." However if there is no such iti ending, the form

insǽn

becomes

insǽn   (by Diphthongization)

and then

inséyn   (by Vowel Shift, Part II)

which is spelled out as *insane* and rhymes with *vain*.

That this is quite a widespread set of processes is suggested by the following sample:

æ̞	é̞
profanity	profane
explanatory	explain

urbanity	urbane
satisfy	sate
ratify	rate
defamatory	defame
panic	pane
pallid	pale
pacify	pace
lacerate	lace
chastity	chaste
banish	bane
cavity	cave
national	nation

As the list should suggest, the process is not just a way of explaining the final sounds of related forms like *chaste* and *chastity*. The words *panic* and *pane* are not related. The list illustrates the operation of a rule relating an underlying ǽ to two different surface manifestations, just as an underlying ę́ was related to two different surface manifestations. Since our alphabet has no letter æ, the letter a̲ is used to represent underlying æ. English spelling is thus not as perverse as it has seemed. The ę and a̲ spellings, though each stands for more than one pronunciation, represent a deeper kind of unity at the morphological level. The relationship between *profane* and *profanity* is reflected in the spelling. It would be less recognizable with a more phonetic spelling system; *profeyn* and *profænity*, for instance.

But we have not yet exhausted the kinds of application of the second part of the Vowel Shift Rule. Not only does it change [+ low] to [− low], but it also changes [− low] to [+ low]. So the vowel ę́, which is

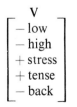

becomes

$$\begin{array}{c} V \\ \begin{bmatrix} + \text{ low} \\ - \text{ high} \\ + \text{ stress} \\ + \text{ tense} \\ - \text{ back} \end{bmatrix} \end{array}$$

or ǽ. By a special rule ǽ becomes [+ back] á̰ in front of the glide y (and ó̰, the corresponding back vowel becomes non-back ǽ in front of w).

Remember the first part of the vowel shift rule converted divíyn into divéyn, with a [− low] [− high] vowel. Now this éy can become an ǽy by the second part of the rule, and then áy. So the form generated is diváyn, whose last syllable rhymes with *mine*.

Forms with underlying ḛ undergo only the first part of the vowel shift rule. But forms with underlying ī must undergo, *in order*, both parts of the rule. The second part might seem a very contrived piece of machinery to make divéyn work out as diváyn, were it not that it is also needed to account for the *insanity*/*insane* kind of vowel alternation.

Of course "divinity" and "divine" are not the only words to undergo the rule application just described. Here are some others:

í	áy
ignition	ignite
derivative	derive
mineral	mine
signature	sign
division	divide
derision	deride
supervision	supervise
inclination	incline
inspiration	inspire
written	write
ridden	ride
opinion	opine
villain	vile
criminal	crime

Now for one final look at the Vowel Shift Rule:

Vowel Shift Part I

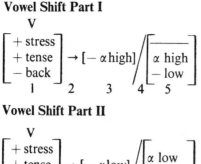

Vowel Shift Part II

The first item in the Part I rule is the same as that in the Part II rule. Since both parts of the rule are about stressed, tense, non-back, non-round vowels, it makes sense to collapse the rules somewhat:

Vowel Shift

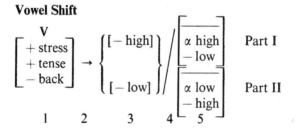

The two parts within the curly braces must still, of course, be applied in the correct order if all the surface pronunciations discussed are to be accounted for.

In fact the Vowel Shift Rule is more general still, and can account for other phenomena that we have not been able to discuss here.

The rounded back vowels ū̧ as in *lute*, ǫ́ as in *boat* and ɔ̄́ as in *bought* undergo the same process (with any resulting ɔ̄́w changing to ā́w). All three back vowels are both [+ back] and [+ round], just as all three "front" vowels are both [− back] and [− round]. Since the α symbol is already in use for the high and low features, we could use a β to stand for the identity of value, whether plus or minus of the back and round features. So the first item in the Vowel Shift Rule could be broadened thus:

$$
\begin{array}{c}
\text{V} \\
\left[\begin{array}{ll}
+ & \text{stress} \\
+ & \text{tense} \\
\beta & \text{back} \\
\beta & \text{round}
\end{array}\right]
\end{array}
$$

Now such alternating pronunciation as *verbose* and *verbosity,* *harmonious* and *harmonic, oppose* and *opposite* can be accounted for in much the same manner as the alternations discussed earlier, and also, with the help of other phonological rules of English, pairs like *profound* and *profundity, abound* and *abundant, reduce* and *reduction,* plus other more complex interactions with alternating consonants. The diversity of English spellings can be shown to reflect important underlying regularities.

In a like way, the Vowel Reduction Rule converting unstressed vowels to schwa, shows how the sound ǝ comes to be spelled a̱ in *spontaneity* and *ability,* e̱ in the last vowel of *element,* i̱ in *opposite,* o̱ in the second vowels of *photograph* and *oppose,* and u̱ in *industry,* and *illustrate.* The existence in related forms of the unreduced vowels in stressed position provides relevant evidence, for example *spontáneous, áble, eleméntary, oppositional, photógraphy, oppóse, indústrial, illústrative.*

Many who deplore the apparent chaos of English orthography fail to see that revising it thoroughly to make it more phonetically regular might result in the destruction of many of the productive visual links between morphologically and semantically related groupings of words, not to mention the difficulties caused by dialect differences. This is not to deny that there are any advantages to any revision of any part of our spelling system. But perhaps the apparent chaos has been overstressed to the detriment of our understanding of the underlying regularities. The orthography is a revealing and economical one for native speakers of English, who do not need all the pronunciation rules required by, say, a Japanese student learning English. Moreover it seems likely that greater exploitation of morphological relatedness could lead to better spelling instruction.

Indeed we have seen how the following pairs may be related to each other:

e̱y as in *mate* and æ̱ as in *mat*
i̱y as in *meet* and e̱ as in *met*
a̱y as in *kite* and i̱ as in *kit*
o̱w as in *note* and a̱ as in *not*
y̱uw as in *cute* and ʌ̱ as in *cut*

Now note how the conventional names for the capital letters A E I O U match the sounds on the left-hand side, while those on the right match the names given to the corresponding lower-case letters in old-fashioned schools. In fact we might well do as Chomsky and Halle did in their great work on English phonology and use the capital letters instead of representation like é̱y and í̱y, and perhaps also use the "regular" values for lower-case letters. So our list would look like this:

mAt	mat
mEt	met
kIt	kit
nOt	not
cUt	cut

Chomsky and Halle *(The Sound Pattern of English*, p. 184) sum up very well what has been discussed here in a footnote to their discussion of di̱vIn, se̱rEn, and pro̱fAn:

> Notice, incidentally, how well the problem of representing the sound pattern of English is solved in this case by conventional orthography. Corresponding to our device of capitalization of a graphic symbol, conventional orthography places the symbol *e* after the single consonant following this symbol ([e] being the only vowel which does not appear in final position phonetically). . . . In this case, as in many other cases, English orthography turns out to be rather close to an optimal system for spelling English. In other words it turns out to be rather close to the true [systematic] phonological representation, given the nonlinguistic constraints that must be met by a spelling system, namely, that it utilize a unidimensional linear representation and that it limit itself essentially to the letters of the Latin alphabet.

Reaching Out

Transformational Analysis and the Study of Style

The object of this essay is to examine some consequences for the total meaning of a literary work of choosing one syntactic medium rather than another. In some sense, the writer "chooses" the particular syntactic form of each sentence of his work and his choices help determine what I shall loosely call the **total impact**. This is not to claim that choices are conscious and deliberate. In fact, as I shall show later, an explicit awareness of syntactic resources is not necessarily advantageous. Nor is there necessarily a one-to-one relation between sentence forms and their stylistic impact.

Literary critics have, for the most part, paid too little systematic attention to syntax. Those who have paid close attention to the verbal "texture" of either prose or poetry seem to have started with a level of word-analysis and then moved straight into thematic analysis. Northrop Frye, for example, distinguishes literary language as language in which

> ... the ... direction is inward, or centripetal, in which we try to develop
> from the words a sense of the larger verbal pattern they make. . . .[1]

but the larger verbal pattern, in Northrop Frye's work, is supra-syntactic. The important syntactic level is rarely touched upon. This omission probably arises from both a lack of knowledge of recent major advances in syntactic theory and a lack of interest in the subject. It is our contention that an awareness of the syntactic

---

[1] Northrop Frye, *Anatomy of Criticism* (Princeton, N. J., Princeton University Press, 1951), pp. 73–74.

choices available to the writer and knowledge of the particular repercussions of each choice should play an important, though not necessarily crucial, role in the critical examination of literary language.

But apart from the more obvious semantic effects resulting from subject-object relationships and the like, how are supposedly significant syntactic choices to be related to larger thematic issues? How does the choice of one syntactic form affect the total impact of a literary work? The relation between form and theme sometimes seems quite simple. Take, for example, the opening of the *Prologue* to Chaucer's *Canterbury Tales*:

> Whan that Aprill with his shoures soote
> The droghte of March hath perced to the roote,
> And bathed every veyne in swich licour,
> Of which vertu engendred is the flour;
> Whan Zephirus eek with his sweete breeth
> Inspired hath in every holt and heeth
> The tendre croppes, and the yonge sonne
> Hath in the Ram his halve cours y-ronne,
> And smale foweles maken melodye,
> That slepen al the nyght with open yë,
> (So priketh hem nature in hir corages);
> Thanne longen folk to goon on pilgrimages . . .

Chaucer is focusing on the coming of spring as a particular but recurrent point in time when life begins to reawaken. He does this in a series of "when" clauses whose subjects are the causers of the awakening: "Aprill," "Zephirus" (the West Wind), "the yonge sonne" (sun). The long series of subordinate clauses climaxes in the highest (or main) clause, which both echoes and rounds off the earlier "when's" with a resounding "then." Corresponding fairly closely to this hierarchical syntactic structure is a hierarchical ordering of the natural elements which figure in this drama of awakening. The ordering goes from the natural elements—showers, wind and sun—to the vegetable world—flowers, and "tendre croppes" (shoots)—to "smale foweles," and finally, in the main clause, to the "folk." Significantly these "folk" long to go on "pilgrimages," this last word suggesting a yet higher order, the divine one.

But although the order is an ascending one, the parallel structuring of the clauses, from the most embedded to the highest clause, emphasizes what all share. All men share this great upsurge of spring life. Man's fidgety desire to go on pilgrimages, lofty as it might seem in isolation, is somewhat humorously related to the springtime restlessness of all life. All suffer from the great itch. Man is very much a harmonious part of this great chain of being. His position is a sure one—below God but above the animals, as the hierarchical ordering of the syntax implies.

This sense of stability in an all-important hierarchy of life is all the more obvious when contrasted with the unease of the opening of the great April poem of this century, T. S. Eliot's "The Waste Land":[2]

> April is the cruellest month, breeding
> Lilacs out of the dead land, mixing
> Memory and desire, stirring
> Dull roots with spring rain.
> Winter kept us warm, covering
> Earth in forgetful snow, feeding
> A little life with dried tubers.
> Summer surprised us, coming over the Starnbergersee
> With a shower of rain; we stopped in the colonnade,
> And went on in sunlight, into the Hofgarten,
> And drank coffee, and talked for an hour.

Here man is no longer in harmony with nature, though ironically, he is more explicitly equated in the metaphoric structure: ". . . stirring dull roots . . . feeding . . . with dried tubers." Spring and summer are neither expected nor desired. Far from being in harmony with the seasons, man is "surprised" by summer. And where, in Chaucer's poem, the new movement spurs man into affirmation through pilgrimage, here the activities are random, purposeless: stopping in the colonnade, drinking coffee, talking for an hour. Eliot's lines lack the tight hierarchical ordering of the earlier poem. Statements are made and then participial phrases expand on the

[2]From "The Waste Land" in *Collected Poems 1909–1962* by T. S. Eliot, copyright 1936 by Harcourt Brace Jovanovich, Inc.; copyright © 1963, 1964 by T. S. Eliot. Reprinted by permission of Harcourt Brace Jovanovich, Inc. and Faber and Faber, Ltd.

statements, with none of the powerful forward movement of Chaucer's *Prologue*. The culminating activities are anti-climactic, trivial, and without purposeful ordering: "stopped . . . and went on . . . And drank coffee, and talked for an hour." And the conjoining with "and's" emphasizes the lack of hierarchical ordering. All this is not to suggest that Eliot's work is inferior. It is, in fact, a powerful expression of dissatisfaction with an aimless, rootless, and orderless world, a dissatisfaction arising from values not so different from those that Chaucer was able to take for granted.

But here an important question arises. The syntactic format of each passage is admirably in harmony with its thematic elements. Is a hierarchically organized sentence form necessary to express in the most effective way the character of a hierarchically ordered universe? And correspondingly are the superficially aimless syntactic forms in the Eliot passage necessary for such a poem? Obviously this cannot be properly answered without the evidence of thematically similar but syntactically different literary works. Even without them, however, it should be obvious that the syntax does not *have* to reflect the thematic content in the ways described above.

So far we have been using a rather impressionistic syntactic approach that is not too different from the methods of the "New Critics." It is time to get down to a more precisely defined analysis of the relation of form to meaning. The problem is that there exists no satisfactory definition of meaning and no likelihood of arriving at one in our present state of knowledge. But we can make some reasonable statements about kinds of meaning especially relevant to literary analysis. We might rather arbitrarily focus on two types of meaning: **basic meaning** and **surface meaning**. **Basic meaning** is, roughly, the meaning that two (or more) paraphrases of a sentence have in common. Synonymy, the basic identity of meaning between two or more utterances, is found in any language. For example, in languages having both active and passive constructions, there is, for almost every passive sentence, an active one with the same basic meaning. In both of these sentences:

(1) It would be picked over at night by the rats with their twitching snouts.

(2) At night the rats would pick it over with their twitching snouts.   Maureen Duffy, *The Paradox Players*

the same creatures are doing something. They are carrying out exactly the same kinds of actions under exactly the same kinds of conditions. What would be true for one sentence must be true for the other. The same truth conditions hold.

But at another level, no two distinct sentences can be paraphrases of each other. A part of the full meaning of any sentence is communicated by the form chosen for the sentence. As the maxim goes, "It's not just *what* you say; it's *how* you say it." If the basic meaning of a sentence is equivalent in a very loose sense to "what you say," then "how you say it" provides what we shall refer to as the **surface meaning**, the extra dimension of meaning communicated by the **style** of the writer. The skilled writer is aware, often without fully realizing it, of a number of alternative ways to express a basic meaning. This is better explained by another illustration.

When George Eliot was working on the manuscript of her novel *Middlemarch*, she first wrote this sentence about a Captain Lydgate:

(3) He had never thought what it would be to borrow.

But then she revised it to read this way:

(4) He had never thought what borrowing would be to him.

George Eliot made a choice between two basically synonymous strings of words. But to George Eliot they cannot have been fully synonymous. Perhaps she felt that the borrowing idea should not appear at the end, where it seems to dominate the sentence. Phrased the original way, the sentence almost demands a hesitation, a pause, before "to borrow," as if borrowing were an unspeakable activity. Presumably the author did not want this degree of prominence for the borrowing idea. Instead the important end position is given to "him." The grammatical subject "borrowing" is still important as the subject of the sentence.[3] The result is that emphasis has been placed on the incongruity, from Captain Lydgate's point of view, of *his* being in a situation where borrowing might be necessary.

---

[3]In fact the use of the *-ing* form *borrowing* rather than the infinitive *to borrow* is quite significant. The infinitive suggests less reality than the more active sounding *-ing* form. To take a clearer example, the sentence "Soames did not like to give in" makes no assumption that Soames did in fact give in. But "Soames did not like giving in" more easily suggests that Soames had really given in, though he had not liked it.

Lydgate's horror culminates with the final "him." The world of borrowing, previously a despised, alien one, has now taken over even *him*! So two sentences with the same basic meaning have as a result of their differing forms additional meaning. Style, the use of one form rather than another, may provide an important kind of meaning. Since this results from the surface form of a sentence, it is called here **surface meaning.** The distinction between **basic meaning** and **surface meaning** is an artificial but nevertheless useful one.

Now a consideration of the stylistic effects of particular surface forms will in a transformational analysis involve consideration of at least some of the transformations relating what we have labeled as **basic meaning** to the alternative surface meanings. What kinds of effects are the result of the application of the **passive transformation** or the **relative clause reduction** rule, or **indefinite deletion**? Since we are not here concerned with linguistic theory, we will ignore current questions as to the status and form of these rules and will treat these transformations as expressing important relations between sentences. So where the **passive transformation** is applied to the structure underlying the relative clause in

(5) The small tables, which someone purchased cheaply from a cafeteria, . . .

the result is:

(6) The small tables, which were purchased cheaply by someone from a cafeteria, . . .

If the **indefinite deletion** rule had also been applied the result would have been:

(7) The small tables, which were purchased cheaply from a cafeteria, . . .

And the **relative clause reduction transformation** would have removed the relative pronoun and the copula:

(8) The small tables, purchased cheaply from a cafeteria, . . .

With these transformations in mind, look now at two passages, one of them from John Updike's novel *The Poorhouse Fair*, which has as its setting an old people's home.

They ate in groups of four at small square tables of synthetic marble which someone had purchased cheaply from a cafeteria that was discarding them. The rain which was falling across the windows, which were high from the floor, had the effect of sealing in light and noise . . . Hook made haste to be among the first to enter their common sitting room, Andrews's old livingroom, which someone had furnished in black leather and equipped with a vast cold fireplace.

They ate in groups of four at small square tables of synthetic marble purchased cheaply from a cafeteria that was discarding them. The rain falling across the high windows, high from the floor, had the effect of sealing in light and noise . . . Hook made haste to be among the first to enter their common sitting room, Andrews's old livingroom, furnished in black leather and equipped with a vast cold fireplace.

John Updike, *The Poorhouse Fair*

Updike's version reveals a careful suppression of any mention of individual human beings who are not inmates and a de-emphasizing of actions which must have been taken by individuals outside the institution. The old people have thus taken on the roles of outcasts acted upon by anonymous, depersonalized institutional entities. One skillful interpolation of the author's voice throws into perspective through its conversational idiom the anonymous inhumanity which seeks to dehumanize the old people.

In the first version, the first relative clause contains a mention of a "someone" who has made an economical purchase for the home:

(9) . . . which someone had purchased cheaply . . .

If the passive transformation alone is applied, shifting the agent phrase from the subject position, the focus of the clause is shifted further from the unspecified person to the cheap tables at which the people sat.

(9)*a* which had been purchased cheaply by someone . . .

The focus is less on what someone did about the tables and more on the tables, which themselves become symbols of a general lack of human concern. The further deletion of the agent phrase subordinates still more the earlier purchasing event and removes any mention of individual human agency. The third step, **relative clause**

reduction, reduces the original purchase to the level of an apparently unimportant detail assigned to a mere participial phrase.

   (9)*b* purchased cheaply . . .

But both passages share the relative clause in

   (10) . . . a cafeteria that was discarding them . . .

Why did not Updike convert this into

   (11) . . . a cafeteria discarding them . . .

If we assume, as we have been assuming so far, that reduction from clause status to participial status involves a reduction of emphasis, then we can infer that, among other considerations, the discarding event is still intended to have some prominence. The tables, like the old people who use them, are unwanted, discarded as useless. Since an institution, "a cafeteria" rather than a person, has discarded them, mention of this non-human agent is retained in the sentence. The thrifty individual bargain-hunter has disappeared while the purchasing act has served to introduce another impersonal institution, one that uses shoddy little fake marble tables.

The same transformations are used later to eliminate any mention of an outside human being who must have arranged the furnishing of the sitting room. The clause

   (12) . . . which someone had furnished in black leather . . .

is reduced by the same set of transformations: **passive**, **agent deletion**, and **relative clause reduction** to

   (13) . . . furnished in black leather . . .

One more straightforward case of relative clause reduction is seen in the conversion of

   (14)*a* . . . rain which was falling across . . .

into

   (14)*b* . . . rain falling across . . .

which seems to be both a matter of euphony and focus. The focus is primarily on the causative relation between the falling rain and its "sealing in" effect. The falling of the rain, expressed in its reduced syntactic phrase, is less of an assertion and more of a descriptive detail.

However, one other difference between the two passages is not so easily described. It is far from obvious that the phrase

(15) . . . the windows, high from the floor . . .

is derived from the structure underlying

(16) . . . the windows, which were high from the floor . . .

The reduced clause, if we accept the reduction analysis, is what was earlier a non-restrictive relative clause, related earlier still to something like

(17) . . . the high windows—and by "high" I mean "high from the floor" . . .

The final reduced version still retains the very human interpolated remark feeling about it, although no human speaker appears in the surface form. It's almost as if someone were saying, "I want you to understand just how it was." Of course the height of the windows from the floor would prevent the old people from being able to look outside while they ate. The inmates are thus very much shut off from the world outside. It's hardly surprising later in the book that when the outside world impinges on them briefly, both the inmates and the outsiders are momentarily terrified.

The transformations discussed—passivization, indefinite deletion, and relative clause reduction—have had two effects:

1. They shift thematically important constituents to syntactic positions which receive focus.
2. They remove entirely or background thematically distracting elements.

The background effect is especially interesting. In many cases the backgrounding involves a kind of presuppositional effect—taking some events for granted rather than asserting them. This is observable in the contrast between the following paragraphs:

The waves crashed. The wind howled. The lifeboat rocked perilously. All this drove us into a state of frenzied terror.

The crashing of the waves, the howling of the wind, and the perilous rocking of the lifeboat all drove us into a state of frenzied terror.

The first three sentences of the first passage correspond to nominalized elements of the single sentence in the second passage. As far as style is concerned the passages are not qualitatively different so long as we assume the goal of each to be different and to fit in appropriately with the larger discourse of which it would be a part. The first, unnominalized passage retains an immediacy lacking in the second one. The writer is asserting the fact of each of the series of events. The cumulative effect of the series leads to a statement of the results of the group of events. But the second passage focuses far more strongly on the causal relation between the behavior of the waves, wind, and lifeboat and the state of mind of the lifeboat occupants. The nominalizations have the effect of backgrounding the events they describe, removing their immediacy and making them members of a more abstract class of events. The presuppositional effect is obvious enough. The events are not asserted to have happened. They are presupposed as having happened, taken for granted.

One author who appears to have consciously exploited the focus and presuppositional properties of transformations is James Baldwin. Baldwin seems especially adept at using the passive and pseudo-cleft processes to highlight thematically important constituents and the relations between them, and sometimes to exploit the presuppositional implications of certain syntactic forms. The **pseudo-cleft transformation** is particularly useful. The two sentences below share the same basic semantic content but differ as to focus and presupposition:

(18) What destroyed the lecture hall was the loud sneeze.

and

(19) What the loud sneeze destroyed was the lecture hall.

The **pseudo-cleft sentence transformation**, though preserving logical synonymy, does focus attention on the particular noun phrase shifted to the end. In (18) the focus is on the loud sneeze, whereas in (19) the focus is on the lecture hall. Moreover in (18) it is **presupposed** that something has destroyed the lecture hall. This fact is taken for granted and the burden of the sentence is on the cause of the destruction. But in (19) the presupposition is that the loud sneeze has destroyed something and the sentence focuses on what was destroyed. Pseudo-cleft sentences, like passives, can be very useful.

Look now at two passages which exploit these transformations to achieve interesting surface effects to create a style with its own meaning. The two passages are basically synonymous. But the choices made between alternative transformations result in the additional dimension of meaning that we have called surface meaning. Style is the result of linguistic choice and surface meaning is the result of style.

> And yet, that there *was* something which all black men held in common became clear as the debate wore on. They held in common their precarious, their unutterably painful relation to the white world. They held in common the necessity to remake the world in their own image, to impose this image on the world. . . . The vision of the world, and of themselves which other people held would no longer control them. In sum, black men held in common their ache to come into the world as men.

> And yet, it became clear as the debate wore on, that there *was* something which all black men held in common. . . . What they held in common was their precarious, their unutterably painful relation to the white world. What they held in common was the necessity to remake the world in their own image, to impose this image on the world, and no longer be controlled by the vision of the world and of themselves, held by other people. What, in sum, black men held in common was their ache to come into the world as men.
>
> James Baldwin, *Nobody Knows My Name*

Both passages are concerned with a particular state of mind common to all black men, it is claimed. In the past, blacks have been acted upon rather than acting on others; they have accepted a view of life formulated by others and have thereby been emasculated. Because of this they share the need to assert themselves as men by reversing the older passive relationship.

The first sentence of the first passage is hard to digest because the writer has chosen not to extrapose:

> (20) And yet, that there was something which all black men held in common became clear as the debate wore on.

The use of the **extraposition transformation** in the second passage yields a more readable alternative:

> (21) And yet, it became clear as the debate wore on, that there *was* something which all black men held in common.

What about the rest of the first passage? The **pseudo-cleft sentence transformation** could have been used to focus on the object noun phrase of each verb by shifting each noun phrase to the end of its sentence, right after the copula. This spotlights the noun phrases:

1. "their precarious, their unutterably painful relation to the white world"
2. "the necessity to remake the world in their own image"
3. "their ache to come into the world as men"

These show a mounting scale of desired activity, culminating in that desired state of coming "as men." The pseudo-cleft versions should enhance this with structures like:

1. What they held in common was their precarious . . .
2. What they held in common was the necessity to . . .

This is what has happened in the second passage. The second and third sentences of the first passage already have nicely parallel subjects and verbs, but the fourth sentence has the blacks consigned to the object position at the end of a long sentence. In the second passage, the passive transformation reverses the subjects and objects of this sentence without changing the sense. Now *they* is the subject and the long noun phrase beginning "the vision . . ." is the object:

> (22) They would no longer be controlled by the vision of the world and themselves which other people held.

Since the second, third, and fourth sentences all have *they* as subject, they can be joined together with an *and*. But since the new sentence would be rather long, the writer preferred just to conjoin the third and fourth sentences and keep the parallelism of "what they held in common . . ." So the third and fourth sentences are now one:

> (23) What they held in common was the necessity to remake the world in their own image, to impose this image on the world, and no longer be controlled by the vision of the world and themselves which other people held.

The sentence contrasts the desired black activity in the first half with the past black passivity in the second half. And the active/passive theme is reinforced by active constructions in the first half and passive constructions in the second half. In fact this isn't quite correct since the last clause

(24) which other people held

is, unlike the one in the second passage, still active. So a change to

(25) which was held by other people

and deletion of the unnecessary *which was* (**relative clause reduction**) achieves the final effect.

The second version has greater coherence and strength. The last three sentences each beginning with "what" (suggesting an implied question) end in a powerful series "white world," "other people," and, finally, "men." This last noun emphasizes the normality and humanness of a desire shared not just by blacks or by whites but by all men. Note that the presuppositional effect of the cleft rule modifies the "held in common" idea. The writer takes it for granted that these black men shared the same need, a need which, he implies later, all men share and should therefore understand. To make this powerful plea, James Baldwin used the second of these two versions in his book.

But in one respect Baldwin may have overdone the transformational manipulation. His long penultimate sentence is very cleverly constructed. The two clauses with active verbs "to remake," and "to impose" match the active control desired. They are balanced by the long clause with two passives "be controlled," and "held by other people." This matches the present passive situation of the blacks. But the surface meaning does not quite come through as intended. Readers will find the sentences hard to read because of the conjoining of active and passive verbs, "to impose . . . and no longer be controlled by." It is difficult to shift gears quickly enough in the same sentence to enter smoothly into a world where the previous semantic subject is now the semantic object.

Baldwin's passage is so elaborately structured that the desired message is partially obscured by an additional surface meaning— that the writer is somewhat inappropriately and excessively concerned with the formal design of his sentences. The style is thus no longer an apparently inevitable, and therefore unobtrusive, result of the interaction between the writer and his subject matter.

The present problem with the kind of transformational analysis suggested here is that it is, in practice, impossible to disentangle satisfactorily the syntactically caused effects from those produced by other elements. Form and context still appear to be inseparable but this is only to be expected when there has been so little work on the semantic effects of transformational processes. The current shift in theoretical transformational research to the analysis of some areas of surface meaning holds considerable promise for those interested in establishing the stylistic contribution of syntactic forms. But what is also urgently needed is more plentiful and varied syntactic analyses of texts. Generalizations as to stylistic effects, like any other kind of generalization, are reliable to the degree that they are based on a large enough body of data.

Bibliography

BALDWIN, JAMES. *Nobody Knows My Name*. New York: Dell Publishing Co., 1961.

CHOMSKY, NOAM. "Deep Structure, Surface Structure, and Semantic Interpretation" in Jacobovits and Steinberg (forthcoming). Cambridge, England: Cambridge University Press.

FRYE, NORTHROP. *Anatomy of Criticism*. Princeton, N.J.: Princeton University Press, 1951.

GOLDIN, AMY. "Deep Art and Shallow Art," *New American Review # 4*. New York: New American Library, 1968.

JACOBOVITS, L. and STEINBERG, D., eds. *Semantics: An Interdisciplinary Reader*. Cambridge, England: Cambridge University Press, forthcoming.

JACOBS, R.A. "Focus and Presupposition: Transformations and Meaning," *College Composition and Communication*, Vol. XX, No. 3 (1969), pp. 187–190.

JACOBS, R. A. and ROSENBAUM, P. S. *Readings in English Transformational Grammar*. Lexington, Mass.: Xerox College Publishing, 1970.

———. *Transformations, Style, and Meaning*. Lexington, Mass.: Xerox College Publishing, 1971.

LAKOFF, GEORGE. "On Generative Semantics" in Jacobovits and Steinberg (forthcoming).

OHMANN, RICHARD. "Generative Grammars and the Concept of Literary Style" in Steinmann, M., *New Rhetorics*. New York: Charles Scribner's Sons, 1967.

UPDIKE, JOHN. *The Poorhouse Fair*. New York: Alfred A. Knopf, Inc., 1965.

WATT, IAN. *The Rise of the Novel*. Harmondsworth, England: Penguin Press, 1963.

Syntax and Language Change

Transformational linguists have shown considerable interest in theories of language change. We all know that languages change, but is there any general direction of change in human languages? Is it possible, for example, to claim that no language will ever undergo one kind of logically feasible change or that one type of change will inevitably be followed by a certain different type of change? And how does the change actually come about? After all, no one woke up one morning to find out that

> ne meaht ðu hine nemnan man[1]

had become

> thou ne mayst nat wene that he be a man

or that the latter had become

> thou mayst not suppose him a man.

And surely linguistic change must have something to do with the child's acquisition of language.

How does a human being learn so quickly to create and understand new sentences in his language, sentences he has never heard before? We can presently make only some rather vague statements. Unlike other animals, the child is innately equipped to produce and

---

[1] The symbol ð ("eth") is the old one usually used for the first consonant sound in *think*. The symbol þ ("thorn") is the one usually used for the first consonant sound in *that*. However there is considerable variation in the spelling of the forms.

understand language. Both the nature and arrangement of the speech organs and, as far as can be determined, the structure of the human brain and neural system, shape the kind of language he will be able to speak and understand. The specifications must be broad enough to encompass the range of variation shown in human languages, yet narrow enough to exclude certain logically conceivable processes. For example, even though it is logically conceivable, no human language forms a passive-type sentence by reversing the order of the words in an active-type sentence.

The small child hears utterances all around him (a relatively small number however), and then, rather than just imitate the utterances, he puts the elements together in different ways to produce utterances he has not previously heard. It's almost as if the child is constructing a theory as to what a correct utterance is in his environment and testing it in his attempts at communication. Those around the child may either correct the child in some way:

Eric (18 months):	Wan ou'.
Mother:	You wanna go out.
Eric:	Wan go ou'.

or, if they misunderstand, force him to reconstruct his utterance. Either way he revises his theory. By the time the child is five he has, without realizing it, constructed an incredibly full theory of his language, although of course he still has much to learn.

Now as he grows older, some perfectly good utterances cease to be heard so often and others change. Perhaps the word *cool*, previously restricted to temperature reference, becomes less restricted. Perhaps he does not hear the object form *whomever* any more, and so he stops applying to this item the general accusative rule producing *him, whom, me*, etc. when they are objects. This need not mean a major change in his theory. He will still understand *whomever* if he hears it and could probably produce it under appropriate circumstances.

But the child that *he* raises may either not hear the *whomever* at all during his first six years or perhaps hear it so infrequently that he doesn't notice it. Consequently he and others of his generation might formulate a somewhat different theory, one in which the accusative transformation applies only to non-compound forms like *who* and *he*. If he does, the use of *himself* may lead him to reconstruct it as *hisself* or to modify his theory again with regard to personal but not relative pronouns. In fact this kind of extension and limitation of the range of application of transformation is a common one. Some speakers may use *who* throughout, others may use *whom* as the object pronoun in relative clauses but not in questions. Others may use *whom* for both questions and relative clauses.

This is roughly the model of change first postulated by such linguists as Morris Halle and Edward Klima in the late fifties and early sixties. The child creates a new theory of the language around him, one likely to be different from the theories of the speakers around him. When he is older, changes in the language really act as rather low-level rules, or perhaps as exceptions which are marked in his "mental dictionary." The next generation may organize its theories somewhat differently, so that an adult rule with exceptions is re-analyzed as a different kind of rule. For example, imagine that in some language the verbs for *think, say, declare, state, believe, doubt* all take a particular kind of clause after them. Then, perhaps because of influence from speakers of a prestigious foreign language, *say, declare,* and *state* come to allow an alternative kind of clause to follow, one already used elsewhere in the grammar. The adult's knowledge might be represented by adding an extra statement to the "dictionary-reading" for each of these verbs. But a child exposed to such an adult, say to one who now uses the older form infrequently, may formulate a general rule distinguishing mental process verbs like *think* from utterance verbs like *say,* or possibly he might abstract some quite different common feature characterizing all constructions using one kind of clause in opposition to constructions using the other kind. Thus over centuries and centuries a language changes, even if the invention of processes like printing slow it down somewhat.

In fact the process of change is more complex since the parent-to-child relationship is only one of many that a child experiences even in his earliest years. This is most obvious, of course, in English-speaking children whose parents are, say, from Portugal. Nevertheless this model of change has proved to be a useful and productive one for the study both of language-acquisition and language change.

In his thesis on diachronic syntax and in an article drawing from it, Edward Klima, a pioneer in the application of transformational methods to historical syntax, showed that it was not always or even often necessary to use different transformations to represent different stages in a language. One could use the same deep structures and the same sets of transformations and still produce different forms if the transformations were applied in different orders.[2]

Here is a somewhat artificial example. Suppose the dialect of an adult-speaker allows these sentences:

(1) I spoke with some man.
(2) The man with whom I spoke met me when I accidentally bumped into him as he looked in a store window.
(3) The man whom I spoke with. . . . (etc.)

One rule relevant here appears to convert pronouns like *who, I, he* into their accusative forms *whom, me, him* when they follow either prepositions or verbs. We'll call this the **Accusative Transformation**. Another shifts prepositions with objects or just objects to the front of a relative clause, for example *I spoke with some man ⇒ some man I spoke with*, and **I spoke with whom ⇒ with whom I spoke* or *whom I spoke with*. Call this the **Fronting Transformation**.

Since the *whom* in sentence (3) does not occur after either a preposition or a verb, we might just consider inventing a new transformation to create this kind of form or, better, add a new environment for the rule, saying that after prepositions and verbs and immediately before noun phrases in relative clauses, pronouns become accusative. But this is not really necessary. If the transformations are ordered, that is have to be applied in only one order, there is no need to add an additional rather complicated environment. The ordering is

1. Accusative Transformation
2. Fronting Transformation

So, by the Accusative Transformation *I spoke with who* becomes *I spoke with whom*. Then, by the Fronting Transformation, this becomes *with whom I spoke* or *whom I spoke with*.

First suppose the man changes his speech habits after some years. Instead of the third sentence above, he says

(3) The man who I spoke with. . . .

---

[2]See especially Klima, Edward S., "Relatedness Between Grammatical Systems," *Language*, Vol. 40, No. 1 (January–March, 1964), pp. 1–20.

This change may be just a simple process reducing *whom* to *who* if it is the first word in the clause. He may still, for example, say *Him I like* once in a while, showing that his grammar has changed very little.

Now suppose that his child picks up the new set of sentences and others like them, but, because of their infrequency, doesn't acquire sentences like *Him I like*. Although his sentences may be of the same kind, he formulates a simpler grammar, differing in the order of the transformations:

1. Fronting Transformation
2. Accusative Transformation

With this ordering we don't need an additional rule reducing *whom* to *who* nor do we even need to expand the environment for the Accusative Transformation. The Fronting Transformation can now convert

> . . . I spoke with who . . .

into either of these:

> . . . with who I spoke . . .
> . . . who I spoke with . .

Then the Accusative Transformation, which applies only to pronouns after verbs or prepositions, applies only to the first of these.

Looked at from a broader historical point of view, the change is really a shift from marking pronouns according to their syntactic function, that is as objects, to marking pronouns according to syntactic position.

If, as we stated earlier, the child is likely to arrive at a more general formulation for the same phenomena for which adults use more complex rules, it would seem that languages should get simpler and simpler with time. In fact, they don't. Simplification in one area of the grammar is quite likely to lead to complications elsewhere. Moreover, the child hears several dialects around him and the optimal generalization he creates for himself may actually be more elaborate and complex with respect to any *one* dialect, even though it is a simplification of *all* the dialects he hears.

This is a major point in an interesting paper by Elizabeth Traugott.[3] She illustrates this with an example of a kind of to and fro movement in relative clause formation over the centuries.

In present-day English there is a deletion transformation commonly known (among transformationalists) as **Relative Clause Reduction**. It reduces *the boy who was coming at three* to *the boy coming at three*. Both the relative pronoun subject and the copula verb *be* are deleted.

However, in Anglo-Saxon, the copula was rarely found deleted. **Relative Pronoun Deletion** normally occurred before adjectives and also before the past participle of *hatan* "call," for example:

Ualena wæs gelæred from anum Arrianiscum biscepe Eudonius wæs haten.

(Valena was taught by a certain Arian bishop was called Eudonius.)

By the Middle English period, the relative deletion process had been simplified by allowing the deletion of *any* relative pronoun heading a clause, and this continued up to the eighteenth century. For example, from Shakespeare's *Measure for Measure*:

I have a brother is condemn'd to die.

But by the end of the eighteenth century the current more complex rules had established themselves. Relative pronoun subjects could only be deleted if a form of the copula *be* followed, and then only if the copula were also deleted. However, at the same time other aspects of relative clause formation were simplified.

So we have, Elizabeth Traugott says, a shift from a complex system for relative pronoun deletion to a simple system and then to an even more complex system than the original. The author's conclusion is that phenomena like this suggest that the changes result not from adult innovation followed by a child's simplification (in the next or some later generation), but from the child's restructuring of the rules of the grammar, not necessarily in the direction of

---

[3]Traugott, Elizabeth, "Simplification versus Elaboration in Syntactic Change," a paper presented to the UCLA Conference on Historical Linguistics in the Perspective of Transformational Theory, February 1969.

simplification. However, the author's analysis here appears to be incomplete since she makes no attempt to link the changes described to the other changes in relative clause formation and other areas of the grammar. A deeper analysis might as easily refute as confirm her conclusions.

It is apparent, anyway, that copula deletion is a quite general process, not one limited to relative clause reduction. A complication in the narrower area might correspond to a simplification in a much larger area. To take another example, by the beginning of the Middle English period, word order in subordinate clauses had changed from Subject–Object–Verb (an order still found in Modern German) with some S–V–O clauses, to a fairly firm S–V–O order. This meant that one could usually unambiguously determine the function of an element from its position. Consequently the deletion of relative pronouns was less likely to create ambiguity.

However, by the eighteenth century English had become a language in which a verb could not ordinarily begin a clause (unless it was imperative, of course.) If the subject did happen to be elsewhere in the sentence, something had to fill the initial position:

A boy was in the garden.
*was a boy in the garden.
There was a boy in the garden.
In the garden was a boy.
In the garden there was a boy.

In such circumstances, the later restrictions on relative pronoun subject deletion may well have been a kind of simplification.

As we indicated above, more general considerations may have stimulated the changes. Mrs. Traugott comments on the morphological resemblance of the Anglo-Saxon relative pronouns to the demonstrative pronouns. They had the same forms: *se* for the nominative masculine singular "that one" and for "who;" *þone* for the masculine accusative singular "that one," "whom," and so on. But between the Anglo-Saxon period and the present day there has been considerable change within this system, change which will need to be considered in a more thoroughgoing investigation of relative deletion.

Arlene Berman, for example, claims that all relative clauses are introduced by the indeclinable þe "that," which can then be freely deleted.[4] The relativized element, that is the one replaced in modern English by *who*, *which*, etc., is replaced by the appropriately inflected demonstrative *se* forms. The *se* form could optionally be fronted. Thus, from an underlying clause, in which *pone*, the accusative form of *se*, is at the end:

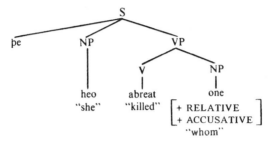

the Fronting Transformation generates

þone þe heo abreat
(whom she killed)

This may optionally be reduced by þe Deletion to

þone heo abreat

However, in the twelfth and thirteenth centuries the forms of the demonstrative *se* undergo changes in which *se* and *seo* are replaced by *þe* and *þeo*, while *þe* or *þat* can replace any of the other forms. So *þe* and *þat* alternated in relative clauses in the twelfth and thirteenth centuries. Now all along, another *þat* had acted as the complementizer in Anglo-Saxon, for example:

Ond ic bebiode on Godes naman þæt nan mon þone æstel from þære bec ne do.

(And I ask in God's name that no man take the board from the book.)

As *þe* ("the") became the regular definite article, the *þat* ("that") supplanted *þe* as a subordination marker both in relative clauses

---

[4]Berman, Arlene, "The Relative Clause Construction in Old and Middle English," in *Report No. NSF-26*, The Computa-Laboratory, Harvard University (Cambridge, Mass., 1970).

and complements. One reason for this is suggested by Miss Berman—once the *se* had changed to *þe*, it was homophonous with the subordinator *þe*. Since the latter was freely deletable and since *se* had not been freely deletable, something had to change. For a time *þe* deletion was avoided, but then both the now complicated rule and the subordinator *þe* were dropped. The uniform use of *þat* for all embedded sentences thus represented a significant simplification in the grammar.

Next, by the fourteenth century the *who/which* inflected relative marker appeared, derived from question and adverbial elements. Sometimes the WH relative occurred together with the subordinator *that*:

> Whan that Aprill with his shoures soote
> The droghte of March hath perced to the roote . . .

> (When April with his sweet showers
> Has pierced to the root the dryness of March,)

From this Miss Berman quite reasonably concludes that the basic transformations were really unchanged, only the forms were different. The emergence of the new WH forms is explained by the author as the result of the ambiguities occurring in S–O–V clauses with the uninflected *that*. She quotes examples in early Middle English in which a relative clause corresponding to

> the girl that the boy saw

could mean either *the girl who saw the boy* or *the girl whom the boy saw*. Therefore a new set of inflected forms was brought in. Of course, once the S–V–O order was firmly established, the accusative inflection of the WH relative pronouns was no longer needed either, and now it is obligatory only after prepositions in most dialects of English. Of course, relative pronoun deletion, where applicable, no longer creates worrisome ambiguities either.

We have not considered the considerable degree of interrelation between the relative pronouns, demonstratives, and the matter of noun-inflection.

The problem is that there is still much more synchronic work to be done. To date we know all too little about the syntax of either Anglo-Saxon or Middle English. This is not to suggest that diachronic work be suspended until the final synchronic analyses come in, for that time will never come. Already there is a major body of knowledge about the syntax of modern English, French, and Spanish. Given fuller syntactic analyses of the earlier stages of these languages, we should at least have taken a major step toward the development of a theory of syntactic change. An analysis of the kinds of syntactic change occurring in human language should suggest some useful hypotheses as to the long-range interactions between speakers, their languages, and the non-linguistic experiences communicated through language.

Dialect Differences and Syntax

Pamela Munro

It seems unlikely that any two speakers of a language would ever agree completely on all questions of usage or pronunciation.[1] But while variations in pronunciation have traditionally been quite sympathetically catalogued, descriptions of dialect differences in syntax have frequently taken the form of prescriptions ("Don't say *ain't!*") following from a norm of "good grammar." As late as 1968, for example, the National Council of Teachers of English published a pamphlet designed to help New York City teachers improve the speech of their disadvantaged pupils, since "every individual who wishes to should have the right and the opportunity to acquire a variety of standard English for the broader access to community life and the surer chance of economic success it will give him." As Sledd (1969), Jacobs (1970), and others have since pointed out, of course, this pamphlet and all such manifestations of the doctrine of "bi-dialectism" side-step the real social issues involved in

---

[1] In traditional terms each speaker has his own "idiolect," and groups of similar idiolects are called "dialects," but this distinction seems to have been lost in modern usage. In almost any case where two or more speakers disagree about even the smallest point of usage, we may say we are dealing with as many dialects as there are opinions. Notice that two speakers who fall into the same dialect relative to the way they construct a certain type of sentence may differ considerably with regard to another unrelated question of syntax (or phonology). Usually the factors which determine what dialect (in the larger sense) a person speaks are cross-cutting: a speaker of "Standard American English" from Nashville is unlikely to speak the same way as another speaker of Standard American English who grew up in San Francisco.

conflicts between groups of people who do not speak the same language.

Transformational grammarians have only recently turned themselves to the task of describing fully the differences in the grammars of different dialects. Until a short while ago, most linguists were concerned with describing only one dialect, either their own or one (often just a construct) representing the majority consensus on acceptability. Dialect differences were frequently dismissed as "exceptions." But linguists have begun to realize that consideration of the way speakers of minority dialects put together sentences often provides valuable insight into the organization of the majority grammar, and may even help to clarify some theoretical questions. The dialect differences considered may be as great as the differences between a New York City NCTE member and her black students, or as small as the differences between two brothers or sisters raised in the same household.

A case where a fairly minor dialect split provides evidence for a theoretical claim currently the subject of some dispute has been described by Guy Carden (1970).

Some linguists, Carden among them, believe that the apparent synonymy of pairs of sentences like

(1) The grammatical sentences in this paper are few.

and

(2) Few sentences in this paper are grammatical.

may be explained by postulating the same deep structure for them. It is claimed that in these and other sentences containing the "quantifiers" *all, many, few*, etc., the quantifier functions as the main verb of the sentence. (Notice that in (1) *(are) few* is the surface structure predicate.) In other words, both (1) and (2) are derived from a structure like (3):

(3)

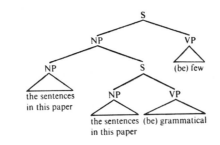

The subject of the main clause of these sentences, then, is the noun phrase *the sentences in this paper*, and the main verb of these sentences is *few*. The subordinate (embedded) sentence *the sentences in this paper are grammatical* functions here something like a relative clause modifying the subject. By applying two different sets of transformations to (3) we can generate the different surface structures (1) and (2).

Now consider the sentence.

(4) All the boys didn't leave.

For some speakers, this sentence means the same as *All the boys stayed* or *None of the boys left*. Others understand it to mean *Not all the boys left*. Still others may find (4) ambiguous between the two readings. These differences in interpretation may be related to the position of the negative element *not* in the deep structure of (4). For the first group of speakers, only the verb phrase *(did) leave* is negated, while, for the second group, it is essentially the quantifier *all* (itself a verb phrase, if we make the assumption discussed above) that is negated.

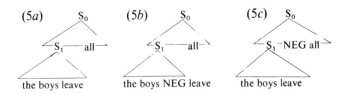

(5*a*) shows the (simplified) structure of the non-negated sentence *All the boys left*. (5*b*) shows the deep structure of (4) for speakers of Carden's first dialect; (5*c*) represents the way (4) is interpreted by speakers of the second dialect. The dialect difference thus depends upon whether the negative (NEG) is inserted into the verb phrase of S_1, as in (5*b*), or of S_0, as in (5*c*).

Now consider the sentence

(6) All the boys didn't leave until six p.m.

It is a rule of English that *until* occurs in the same clause as punctual-action (rather than repeated-action or continuous-action), verbs like *leave* only when there is a negative in that clause too. Thus

(7) *John left until six p.m.

is unacceptable. We would expect, then, that if *until six p.m.* is added to the verb phrase of S_1 in (5), a negative must also be present in S_1 if the output sentence is to be grammatical.

Dialect evidence bears out this claim. Speakers of the first dialect discussed above, for whom *not* is understood as part of S_1, understand (6) unambiguously to mean *All the boys stayed until six p.m.* Speakers of the second dialect, however, who interpret *not* as part of S_0, find (6) ungrammatical. For them, (6) means the same as

(8) *Not all the boys left until six p.m.,

which is ungrammatical for all speakers in the same way that (7) is, since in the deep structure of this sentence *not* and *until* do not occur in the same clause.

The grammar of English must have a rule to explain the rather strange fact that

(9) I don't think the boys left.[2]

can mean the same as

(10) I think that the boys didn't leave.

This rule is often called **negative transportation**, because the negative that semantically belongs in the lower clause of both sentences has somehow been "transported" up into the main clause of (9). One necessary restriction on this rule is that it can only move the negative one sentence up; thus, *I don't think . . .* cannot reflect the deep-structure negation of any clause but the one which stands as the direct object of *think*.

(11) I don't think that the boys who left will catch the train.
(12) I think that the boys who didn't leave will catch the train.

In other words, (11) does not mean the same as (12). The negative in (12) is in the relative clause which is itself subordinate to the clause functioning as the direct object of *think*.

But what if a sentence with a quantifier follows *I don't think that . . .* ?

---

[2]Sentences like (9) also have another reading equivalent to *It is not the case that I think that. . . .*

(13) I don't think that all the boys left.
(14) I think that not all the boys left.
(15) I think that all the boys stayed.

Speakers of all three of the dialects Carden studied stated that (13) could mean the same as (14) but that it could not mean the same as (15). This finding provides twofold support for the claim that quantifiers must be analyzed as separate "higher" predicates. First, if (16)

(16)

or (5a) represents the structure which follows *I don't think* in (13), that negative in the main clause of (13) can have been moved by negative transportation only from S_0, so that *all*, not *leave*, must have originally been negated—as we would expect from the synonymy of (13) and (14). Secondly, if a simple sentence, rather than the complex structure of (16), followed *I don't think*, and if the *not* in (13) were postulated to come from that simple sentence, (13) should be ambiguous in just the way that (4) is—it should be synonymous with (15) as well as (14).

In this analysis, the difference in the way that speakers of three dialects interpret sentences like *All the boys didn't leave* is ascribed to deep structure. For speakers of Carden's first two dialects, this sentence must be derived from two separate deep structures which differ as to the position of the negative; for speakers of the third dialect, it may be derived from either of these two structures.

Elliott, Legum, and Thompson (1969) discovered that transitive relationships may exist between selected pairs of sentences which differ in interpretation or grammaticality between different dialects. They showed that if a person accepts (or rejects) a certain sentence as grammatical, it is often possible to predict that he will also accept (or reject) another related sentence which differs only slightly from the first one.

A group of the experimenters' friends and colleagues were presented with sentences (17)–(20) and asked to judge their grammaticality.

(17) Sophia Loren was seen by the people while enjoying herself.

(18) The people saw Sophia Loren while enjoying themselves.

(19) Judy was seen by the people while enjoying themselves.

(20) The people saw Karen while enjoying herself.

In each of these sentences the subject of *(was/were) enjoying* has been deleted after *while*. These deleted subjects in each case name the same person as ("are coreferential with") one of the nouns in the preceding main clause. In (17) and (18) the deleted nouns correspond to the subjects of the main clauses; in (19) and (20) the nouns corresponding to the objects are deleted. In addition, in (17) and (19) the main clause is passive, while in (18) and (20) it is active. The experimenters hypothesized first, that most speakers would favor subject-deletion after *while* when the main clause is a passive, and second, that a good many speakers would have a constraint in their grammars precluding such deletion except when the deleted subject is coreferential with the subject of the main clause. In other words, the sentences should decline in acceptability from (17) to (20).

That was exactly what happened. The subjects' varying responses split them up into five separate dialects, as shown in (21), where + and − indicate acceptance and rejection respectively.

(21)

		Sentences			
		(17)	(18)	(19)	(20)
Dialects	1	+	+	+	+
	2	+	+	+	−
	3	+	+	−	−
	4	+	−	−	−
	5	−	−	−	−

This sort of pattern has been called an "implicational scale." From the table we can predict with a high degree of accuracy that if someone accepts sentence (20), he will also accept the other three sentences, for example. Similarly, if we know that someone rejects (18), we would suppose that he will also reject (19) or (20).

Such studies as these use information from dialects which are not really very different. None of the interpretations of (4) discussed above would be classed as "substandard," and no one's status as a speaker of Standard American English would be jeopardized solely by his acceptance of (20) or rejection of (17).

But quite similar implicational scales can be constructed to define much further reaching dialect divisions. Six "features" of Jamaican Creole speech were observed by DeCamp to reflect the social hierarchy of seven speakers:[3]

(22)

		Features					
		A	B	C	D	E	F
Speakers	1	+	+	+	+	+	+
	2	+	+	+	+	+	−
	3	+	+	+	+	−	−
	4	+	+	+	−	−	−
	5	+	+	−	−	−	−
	6	+	−	−	−	−	−
	7	−	−	−	−	−	−

(Here, + shows the presence and − the absence of a feature.) These features include such things as choice of English *versus* "native" words—considerations which probably have at least some validity as indicators of whether a person speaks "well" or not. There is a clear social progression from Speaker 7, an illiterate peasant farmer, to Speaker 1, the educated owner of an appliance store. DeCamp's study suggests that, given the information that feature D was present in the speech of a given speaker of Jamaican Creole, we might suppose that his speech would include features A, B, and C as well, and so on.

However, this argument is suspiciously circular.[4] Table (22) leads us to infer that it is the features A, B, C, etc., which determine what social dialect a Jamaican speaks, whereas actually it was the known social standings of the speakers which determined the (arbitrary?) selection of these features. If we begin our analysis with the information that a group of speakers may be rank-ordered on some social scale, it should not be impossible, given a large body of data and a restricted number of speakers, to find an arbitrary set of features which pattern just as in (22). We should probably require the linguist giving such an analysis in definition of a group of social dialects to show that such features are indeed related in some significant way in the grammar.

---

[3]DeCamp, David, "Toward a generative analysis of a post-Creole speech continuum" (paper delivered at the Conference on Pidginization and Creolization of Languages, Mona, Jamaica, 1968). Discussed in Fasold (1970), pp. 552–553, 555.

[4]As Fasold (1970) suggests, pp. 555–556.

Some facts about the way different dialects of English use several sorts of multiple negation have recently been analyzed by William Labov.[5] The ways that three types of multiple negation pattern in three different dialects may be shown in a modified implicational chart, where, as before, + indicates categorical presence of the syntactic feature and − indicates its absence. The asterisk, *, indicates the variable presence of the feature—it occurs in some contexts but not in others.

$(23)^6$ Types of Multiple Negation

		1	2	3
Dialects	1	−	−	−
	2	*	*	−
	3	+	*	*

Dialect 1 is Standard English (no multiple negation); 2 is one nonstandard dialect; 3 is the dialect spoken by black teenagers in Harlem. Notice that the same three dialects will be distinguished if each occurrence of * is replaced by +, but that the formulation of (23) gives us more information about the degree to which these nonstandard syntactic features are present in the various dialects. We can interpret (23) in the same way as (21) and (22): presence of type 2 multiple negation implies presence of type 1 multiple negation, for example. Judging by the increased incidence of type 1 multiple negation in dialects 1 through 3, we might predict that, say, there would be a higher incidence of multiple negation 2 in dialect 3 than in dialect 2. When (23) is revised to show the actual percentages of occurrence of the three types of multiple negation, we see that this is indeed the case:

(24)   Types of Multiple Negation

		1	2	3
Dialects	1	0%	0%	0%
	2	81%	25%	0%
	3	100%	35%	9%

[5]"Negative attraction and negative concord in various English dialects" (paper delivered at the Linguistic Society of America annual meeting, New York City, 1968). Discussed in Fasold, pp. 553–555.

[6](23) appears in Fasold, p. 555, adapted from William Labov, Paul Cohen, Clarence Robins, and John Lewis, *A study of the nonstandard English of Negro and Puerto Rican speakers in New York City*, vol. I, Final report, Coöperative Research Project 3288, U. S. Office of Education (ERIC ED 028 423), p. 277. (23) has been adapted from (24).

The three features considered in (23) and (24) should, theoretically, define a fourth dialect (characterized by absence of multiple negation 2 and 3 and variable presence (less than 81% occurrence) of multiple negation 1). With this exception, however, (23) and (24) work just like (21) and (22) to delineate a range of dialects by a symmetrically patterned configuration of language features. The type of chart illustrated by (24) is more valuable than that illustrated by (22) because, besides showing everything that (22) does, it reveals in addition that features considered substandard are present to a greater degree in socially lower dialects than in socially higher ones.

One of the consistently puzzling features of black English is its characteristic deletion of conjugated forms of the copula *be*. In all varieties of white English, of course, the copula may be very freely contracted (especially when it follows a subject pronoun). Thus *John's here* is generally preferred to *John is here* by white speakers. But in black English the corresponding alternation is usually between *John here* and *John is here*, with *John's here* occurring less often even than the full form. Labov observed in studying black youths in New York City that, in fact, the total percentage of contracted and deleted forms of the copula in any given sample of his subjects' speech closely paralleled the percentage of contracted forms in the (also nonstandard) speech of a control group of white teenagers:[7]

(25)	Black Teenagers		White Teenagers	
	after noun phrase	*after pronoun*	*after noun phrase*	*after pronoun*
% of full forms	45	0	41	1
% of contracted forms	19	23	59	99
% of deleted forms	36	77	—	—

The operations of contraction and deletion in the black group's speech should not be seen as totally unrelated processes. Labov suggests that the grammar of this group contains a rule not found

---

[7]After Labov (1969), p. 730. The "black teenagers" are the Cobras (aged 12–17), speaking in group style; the "white teenagers" are the Inwood control group (aged 10–17), also in group style.

in the white group's grammar, a rule for deleting an already contracted copula. The contraction rule is optional in all varieties of
English; the deletion rule, which, Labov claims, must follow the
contraction rule, is also optional. In other words, a base sentence
like *John is here* may become *John's here* in both dialects (by application of the contraction rule), and may further become *John here*
for black speakers (by application of the deletion rule).

In the usual formulation of rules in a transformational grammar,
those rules that are optional are distinguished from those that are
obligatory, but generally no attempt is made to explain precisely
when an optional rule is likely to apply. The data above clearly
suggest, however, that for both the black and the white groups
the processes of contraction and contraction-and-deletion are much
more likely to occur (in fact are virtually obligatory in this style of
speech) when the verb follows a pronoun rather than a noun phrase.
In similar fashion, whether or not contraction or contraction-and-
deletion will occur is dependent also on what follows the copula:
noun phrases, predicate adjectives, locative expressions, present
participles, and *gonna* (in that order) provide increasingly more
favorable environments for the operation of these rules. Since this
seems to be an important fact about the operation of these rules
in these dialects (and since it suggests that similar environmental
factors could be found to condition the operation of other optional
rules), the grammars we write will be less meaningful if we do not at
least attempt to include statements of such conditioning environments in our rules. Labov has proposed a type of "variable rule"
in which the different combinations of conditioning factors are given
numerical weightings to indicate the relative probability of the rule's
applying in such an environment. This is an innovative and potentially very effective way of making the grammars we write
better predictors of linguistic reality.

Studies like Carden's and that of Elliott, Legum, and Thompson
help us realize the multitude of differences that may exist between
speakers of Standard American English and show how the different
dialects involved may be related. The work of linguists like DeCamp,
Labov, and many others shows how the grammars of minority
dialects differ from the grammar(s) of standard English. All these
studies indicate clearly that dialect evidence must not be ignored in
the formulation of a viable and comprehensive syntactic theory.

Clearly, a related set of grammars which accounts for the facts of many dialects is more powerful than the grammar of any one dialect, prestigious or not. But before this goal can be achieved, linguists and laymen alike must realize that no natural language is "impoverished"; and that anyone's dialect is both a fit subject for research and a fit vehicle for communication.

Bibliography

CARDEN, GUY. "A Note on Conflicting Idiolects," *Linguistic Inquiry*, Vol. 1 (1970), pp. 281–290.

ELLIOTT, DALE, STANLEY LEGUM, and SANDRA ANNEAR THOMPSON. "Syntactic Variation as Linguistic Data," *Papers from the Fifth Regional Meeting, Chicago Linguistic Society* (1969), pp. 52–59.

FASOLD, RALPH W. "Two Models of Socially Significant Linguistic Variation," *Language*, Vol. 46 (1970), pp. 551–564.

JACOBS, RODERICK A. "Review of NCTE 1968," *English Journal*, Vol. 59 (1970), pp. 427–429.

LABOV, WILLIAM. "Contraction, Deletion, and Inherent Variability of the English Copula," *Language*, Vol. 45 (1969), pp. 715–762.

NATIONAL COUNCIL OF TEACHERS OF ENGLISH/BOARD OF EDUCATION OF THE CITY OF NEW YORK. *Nonstandard Dialect*. Champaign, Illinois, 1968.

SLEDD, JAMES. "Bi-dialectism: The Linguistics of White Supremacy," *English Journal*, Vol. 58 (1969), pp. 1307–1315 and 1329.

Linguistic Semantics Today

Paul G. Chapin

Probably few terms cover such a disparate variety of endeavors as "semantics." Poets and philosophers, linguists and logicians are all concerned in one way or another with meaning, and there are as many different kinds of activity which can be called semantics as there are ways of being concerned about meaning. Thus it is necessary to begin even a survey article on semantics by narrowing the focus of discussion. The word "Linguistic" in the title indicates the intended focus; what it includes will become clear shortly, but first let me mention some things it excludes.

In philosophy there are at least two distinguishable senses in which people study semantics. One sense is the study of the properties of the abstract relationship obtaining between a symbol and its referent, a name and the thing it names. Such classical philosophical distinctions as those between denotation and connotation, and between sense and reference, have arisen from this study. The other sense is more technical: it is the study, within formal or symbolic logic, of the rules governing the correspondence between logical formulae and their propositional interpretations. The work of Carnap, Reichenbach and Tarski in this field is best known. Neither of these areas will be discussed here.

"General Semantics" should also be mentioned in passing. This is not so much a field of study as a sort of religion, whose main tenet is that most if not all of the difficulties of the human condition can

SOURCE: Reprinted from *The English Record*, April 1970, by permission of the author and *The English Record*.

be traced to the sloppy use of words and to the uncritical acceptance of the Aristotelian doctrine of the excluded middle. General Semantics was founded by Count Alfred Korzybski, who wrote *Science and Sanity*; its best-known practitioner today is undoubtedly S. I. Hayakawa, now President of San Francisco State College. The relationship of General Semantics to semantics is about the same as the relationship of Psycho-Cybernetics to cybernetics.

The aims of linguistic semantics, as of other branches of linguistics, are both descriptive and theoretical. The descriptive task is to provide an explicit characterization of what it is that the native speaker of a language knows which enables him to judge of words and sentences of that language whether they have the same meaning, or different meanings, or mutually contradictory meanings. To put it differently, the task is to explain what it is that words and sentences in different languages have in common that makes it possible for them to serve as translations of one another. The theoretical task is to make explicit the notion "semantic description of a natural language," that is, to give a universal characterization of the semantic components of particular languages. This would amount to a characterization of the innate structures of the mind which enable a human child to learn to understand and to use in a semantically accurate way any natural language to which he receives a certain amount of exposure.

It is important and frequently difficult in doing semantics to distinguish between knowledge of a language and knowledge about the world. Thus to agree to the truth of the sentence "A bachelor is an unmarried man," we don't need to know any bachelors; we only need to know English. On the other hand, knowing English won't help us decide whether it's true that "Alex Muff lives in Poughkeepsie"; we need to know something about Alex, or something about Poughkeepsie. These cases are simple, but what about "Two times two is five," or "Electromotive force is measured in volts"? Does our denial of the first and our assent to the second depend on our knowledge of English, or on our language-independent knowledge about the world, or on neither? In such cases the line is difficult to draw, but it must be drawn, or else a semantic description of a language must include an encyclopedic description of everything the speaker of that language knows about the world around him, which is an impossible task.

The problems of descriptive semantics can conveniently be divided into two general domains, problems of lexicon and problems of semantic representation of sentences. Problems of lexicon are problems having to do with words, or morphemes, which are the basic building blocks of the language. How may we best describe their internal semantic structures, their similarities and differences, their natural groups? For example, how is "uncle" similar to "aunt," and how to "father"? What do all three words have in common which is not shared by "butcher"? What is the relationship between "potato" and "spud"? Between "hot" and "cold"? Between "cow" meaning "bovine" and "cow" meaning "to awe"? Merely assigning names to these relationships, such as synonymy, antonymy, homonymy, etc., only acknowledges their existence; it doesn't serve to explain or clarify them. A complete semantic description of a language would have to contain a dictionary giving not only exhaustive descriptions of the semantic content of the morphemes of the language, but also giving general principles for comparing the semantic descriptions of morphemes to determine whether they are related in one of the ways discussed above. These principles of comparison would then define precisely the notions of synonymy, antonymy, etc. Some approaches to these problems of lexicon will be discussed below.

The semantic representation of sentences is a problem almost as old as philosophy itself. Classical Aristotelian logic recognized that the kind of semantic classification of sentences needed for constructing rules of valid inference doesn't correspond to any major sort of grammatical classification of the sentences. For the purposes of logic, such fundamental syntactic distinctions as declarative-interrogative or active-passive are much less important than whether the determiner in the subject noun phrase is "all" or "some," a grammatically minor point. Thus some sort of semantic representation is required which is quite distinct from the grammatical representation of sentences. The construction of such representations, at least for the kinds of sentences used in mathematics and the empirical sciences, has been one of the major concerns of modern symbolic logic.

The problem of semantic representation of sentences for the linguist who is working in semantics is different from that which confronts logicians, however. The logician wishes to construct a semantically perfect artificial "language" in which theories and propositions can be expressed clearly and precisely, avoiding the pitfalls of ordinary natural language. The linguist wishes to account for a set of linguistic phenomena. From the logician's point of view, it is inefficient to be able to say the same thing in two different ways, and his logical system would avoid this inefficiency wherever possible. The linguist, on the other hand, recognizes that in natural languages there are sentences which are paraphrases of each other; his semantic descriptions of those languages must accommodate that fact. For the logician, it is intolerable for a single formula to have more than one interpretation; but in natural language ambiguity is rife, and again linguistic semantics must provide an accurate account of the facts.

Other phenomena to be accounted for by linguistic semantics include judgments of semantic anomaly or oddness of particular sentences, such as "My left foot's sister frequently totals eleven" or "Colorless green ideas sleep furiously" (to take an example with a relatively high probability of occurrence in English); judgments that certain sentences are analytic (or contradictory), that is to say, true (or false) by virtue of their meaning alone, such as "His parting words were his farewell utterance" or "My maiden aunt is a married man"; and the contextual disambiguation of words—"bank" taken by itself can mean "the slope by the side of a river" or "an edifice for financial transactions," but the latter meaning would never occur to someone hearing the sentence "He slid down the bank."

American linguists have begun to pay serious attention to these problems only in the last decade. There has been a long tradition of such scholarship in the Soviet Union and other European countries, which has been largely unknown in America (the interested reader is referred to the extensive bibliographies in Weinreich 1963 and Weinreich 1966). Because of the behaviorist orientation of American structuralist linguistics, such problems were generally considered unresearchable. The position taken by Bloomfield in his book *Language* (1933) was the dominant one:

> We have defined the *meaning* of a linguistic form as the situation in which the speaker utters it and the response which it calls forth in the hearer. (p. 139)

The consequence of such a definition is logically inescapable:

The situations which prompt people to utter speech include every object and happening in their universe. In order to give a scientifically accurate definition of meaning for every form of a language, we should have to have a scientifically accurate knowledge of everything in the speaker's world. The actual extent of human knowledge is very small, compared to this. . . . The statement of meanings is therefore the weak point in language study, and will remain so until human knowledge advances very far beyond its present state. (pp. 139–140)

Who could study semantics, believing that success demanded omniscience?

The first decisive break with this sterile tradition was made in the classic paper "On the Semantic Structure of Language," by the late Uriel Weinreich (Weinreich 1963). No summary can possibly do justice to this article, a rich mixture of theoretical machinery and substantive observations such as

There seems universally to be equal or greater discrimination of time distinctions in past than in future. (p. 125)

It seems that no language refers to individual constants of more than one class, e.g. by having "proper verbs" as well as "proper nouns." (p. 129)

. . . the expression of endearment seems to intersect with the designatum of smallness; even if this is not a semantic universal it is quite typical although theoretically it could have been the other way around. (p. 122)

The reader who is bothered by the repeated use of the word "seems" should recognize that Weinreich, well-versed as he was in numerous languages, realized that he was working with a near vacuum of data, as he insists both at the outset:

The scarcity of relevant data is in itself a major obstacle to the elaboration of workable hypotheses. (p. 115)

and at the conclusion:

At many points in the undertaking . . . reference data were felt to be so scant as to make the conclusions unattractively general and modest in relation to the conceptual machinery. (p. 152)

On the theoretical side, Weinreich argued that there are two principal types of operations for combining semantic units into higher-level semantic units. He called these **linking** and **nesting**. The effect of linking is to create a higher-level semantic unit whose properties are a simple compound of the properties of the lower-level units which comprise it. Thus for example "a blue pencil" is something which is both blue and a pencil. Nesting, on the other hand, establishes a more complex relationship among the lower-level units. The sentence "Aloysius broke the poi-jar" doesn't simply describe a situation involving Aloysius, breaking, and a poi-jar, but rather sets these concepts in a definite relationship to each other. Both linking and nesting can occur on several levels, as in "a violent blue vase," where "violent" is an attribute of "blue" but not of "vase," or in "Max heard Sheila swat Monroe," where one of the nested concepts is itself formed by an operation of nesting. Weinreich made the following interesting observation:

> In all languages a combination of signs takes the form of either linking or nesting, and all languages use both patterns in kernel sentences. No further patterns are introduced by transformations. While the number of levels is not theoretically limited, linking on more than three and nesting on more than four is very rare. (p. 134)

The part about kernel sentences and transformations is important, and its meaning will be clearer shortly. The chief criticism to be made of the balance of the comment is that in spite of the examples offered, the notions of linking and nesting are too vague and undefined to give much content to the claim that every language uses just those two semantic operations.

The real importance of Weinreich's paper was not so much in the specific proposals he made, although these have had and will continue to have their influence. It was primarily in the substantive and researchable questions he raised, and in his establishment, or re-establishment, of semantics as a viable and respectable field of linguistic inquiry. Once the right questions are asked, the relevant data can be gathered.

The late '50's and early '60's saw the beginnings of a full-blown revolution in American linguistics, a revolution which by now is virtually complete. It is customary to establish as the starting point the publication in 1957 of *Syntactic Structures*, by Noam Chomsky. In this little book, actually a condensation of a much larger work which has never been published, Chomsky offered compelling reasons for challenging the whole conceptual framework of American structuralist linguistics, and proposed a rich and highly detailed theoretical schema to replace it, with substantial empirical evidence for his position. Chomsky himself regarded semantics as *terra incognita* and sought to establish a clear distinction between syntax and semantics, so that progress in the former field would not be hampered by the mysteries of the latter. However, the impact of his theory was so great that it was inevitable that someone would investigate semantic problems from the vantage point it offered. Such was the background of Katz and Fodor's article "The Structure of a Semantic Theory" (1963).

Katz and Fodor accepted Chomsky's position that "Grammar is best formulated as a self-contained study independent of semantics" (Chomsky 1957, p. 106) and went a step further, to argue that semantics depends on grammar, i.e., syntax. Weinreich advanced a similar argument, but all that he meant by it was that semantics need not concern itself with ungrammatical (syntactically deviant) utterances. Katz and Fodor intended something more. They theorized that semantics is *interpretive*, which is to say, that the semantic representation of any sentence can be uniquely constructed by a set of rules which have only the grammatical structure of the sentence and the meanings of its component words to work on. In this theory, the converse would not hold true; given a semantic representation, you couldn't uniquely determine a grammatical form. An analogy may prove illuminating, even though it is inexact: for any fraction, it is possible to apply a simple formula to compute its representation as a decimal to any desired degree of accuracy— simply divide the denominator into the numerator, carrying out the division to as many places as you wish. However, given a decimal fraction, there is no general formula for computing the regular fraction which it approximates. Thus 3/17 to 16 places is .1764705882352941; but given the latter number, there's no way but trial and error to find that it's a 16-place approximation of 3/17. We could say that the rule for computing decimal representations is an interpretive rule, whose input is a fraction. The input to the rules of semantic interpretation, according to Katz and Fodor, are the grammatical or syntactic structures of sentences, with the meanings of the component words plugged in.

The notion of "grammatical structures of sentences" mentioned above needs some elucidation. One of the most important results of Chomsky's work was to enrich this notion considerably. Earlier, structuralist work in syntax had operated almost entirely within the so-called Immediate Constituent Structure model. The contention was that the structure of a sentence can be described as a hierarchy of higher level constituents composed of lower level constituents, in the form which today is commonly represented by a grammatical "tree." Chomsky demonstrated that one tree is insufficient to describe the structure of a sentence adequately; what is required, rather, is a series of related trees, with the relations between adjacent trees in the series expressed by rules called *transformations* (hence the term *transformational grammar*). For example, an adequate description of English questions could not be given simply by showing the characteristic immediate constituent structure of question sentences. To give a full account, it is necessary also to show the structure of their corresponding declaratives, and to state the transformational rule relating them (this is oversimplified to make the point clear). Chomsky also showed that some sentences require longer series of trees in their descriptions than others; for example, since the description of the declarative is just a part of the description of the corresponding question, the description of the question involves at least one more tree than the description of the declarative. He argued that one could isolate those sentences of a language which have the smallest possible number of trees in their descriptions. These he termed the *kernel sentences* of the language. In English, these are the simple affirmative active declaratives.

At this point, grammatically based semantic analysis begins to make a great deal of sense. If one tries to relate all of the various sentence types and subtypes of a language directly to semantic representations, bewilderment comes quickly. But if one thinks of them as linked by rules to a basic set of sentences, then the problem of semantic interpretation becomes the simpler problem of providing semantic representations for just that basic set, with principles of modification based on the transformational rules as required. Recognition and systematic exploitation of this was Katz and Fodor's basic insight, although the germ of the idea had appeared earlier in the quotation from Weinreich already given.

Katz and Fodor called their rules of semantic interpretation *projection rules*. The basic variety of these, and the variety which they developed in some detail, are rules which apply to the tree structure of a kernel sentence from the "bottom up," amalgamating the readings (semantic representations) of lower level constituents to form the readings of higher level constituents, all the way up to the constituent *Sentence*, at which point the result is a semantic representation of the sentence itself. In general, not all of the readings of lower level constituents survive the amalgamation process, since some of them don't fit each other. Elimination of mutually incompatible readings is one result of the application of the projection rules.

Once again an example is called for. The example Katz and Fodor use is "The man hits the colorful ball." Katz and Fodor assign three readings to "ball": 1) a dance; 2) a toy; 3) a piece of ammunition. "Colorful" has two readings: 1) brightly colored; 2) picturesque; and "hits" two: 1) collides with; 2) strikes with an instrument (there may be other readings for these words, but they are not important to the example). One of the projection rules amalgamates the readings of adjectives and the nouns they modify; in the example sentence this rule will produce a derived reading for "colorful ball" from the readings of "colorful" and "ball." Thus a colorful ball can be a brightly colored dance, or a picturesque dance, or a brightly colored toy, or . . . at this point we run into a problem, since there's something peculiar about referring to a toy ball as "colorful" meaning "picturesque." Only certain sorts of nouns can properly be modified by this adjective; "ball" meaning "dance" is among them, but "ball" meaning "toy" is not. Thus this pair of readings is thrown out by the projection rule. Going to a higher level constituent, another projection rule combines the readings for verbs and their objects, to give a derived reading for a verb phrase. "Hits" in both of its assigned readings requires a physical object as direct object. Thus although "picturesque dance" is one of the readings of the object noun phrase "colorful ball" in isolation, a dance is not a physical object, and this reading is thrown out by the projection rule for verbs and objects. "Brightly colored toy," however, is a reading which survives, and in fact is compatible with both of the readings of "hits." The whole verb phrase thus has two different readings corresponding to the two different readings of "hits" with "colorful ball" meaning "brightly colored toy" as its direct object, but no reading with the "dance" meaning of "ball" as direct object. Finally, projection to the level of the sentence involves amalgamation of the readings for the verb phrase with the readings for the subject noun phrase "the man." None of the surviving readings of the verb phrase is eliminated at this point.

Within this framework it is possible to describe some of the empirical phenomena of linguistic semantics described earlier. Contextual disambiguation is the result of the projection rules' throwing out incompatible readings of constituents. To repeat the earlier example, although in isolation "bank" has a reading "building" as well as "slope by the side of a river," the former reading doesn't enter into the sentence "He slid down the bank"; this is because the verbal complex "slide down" requires some fairly smooth sloping surface as its direct object, and thus the projection rule for verb phrases retains only the appropriate reading of "bank" in deriving the reading of the verb phrase. Semantic anomaly is the limiting case, where *no* readings survive because of violations of constituent compatibility. A sentence is analytic if the readings of its predicate are all contained in the readings of its subject.

Weinreich (1966) attacked Katz and Fodor's projection rule schema on two major points. In his earlier paper (Weinreich 1963), he had argued that there are two kinds of semantic operations, two ways in which semantic readings of constituents combine with each other, which he called linking and nesting. The only kind of semantic combination achieved by Katz and Fodor's projection rules is amalgamation, equivalent to Weinreich's linking. Weinreich considered Katz and Fodor's theory in this respect hopelessly impoverished; in the example discussed, he claimed, it is simply not the case that the semantic relation between "colorful" and "ball" is the same as that between "hit" and "colorful ball."

The second point of attack had to do with Katz and Fodor's "bottom-to-top" method of combining and eliminating readings of constituents. In Katz and Fodor's framework, a word starts out with a certain number of readings; in the course of applying the projection rules, readings can be lost, but new readings can never be added. Thus a word, or any constituent, can never have readings in context which it does not have in isolation. Weinreich argued that in fact it is a fairly normal linguistic phenomenon for a word to gain extra meaning in context. This can happen in several ways. A word may become more specific in context than it is in isolation; for example, "neighbor" is unspecified with respect to sex, but if you say "I have a pretty neighbor," no one believes your neighbor is male. Metaphor is a fairly common linguistic device, not just a poetic device; the verb "kill," for example, is used in quite different (although related) senses when its direct object is an animate object, a mechanical device capable of sustained motion, a short period of time, and a ping-pong ball. It would be difficult to argue that "kill" has all of these senses in isolation. Finally, a special situation may justify an ordinarily anomalous usage, as for example "After he broke his jaw, Bobby Hull had to drink his steaks." In Katz and Fodor's system, such a sentence could receive no full interpretation. Weinreich insisted that the fact that we can make perfectly good sense of it means that an adequate semantic theory must account for it.

To accommodate this objection, as well as the aspects of Katz and Fodor's theory which he considered correct, Weinreich proposed an alternative schema for semantic interpretation. Weinreich's model involved developing semantic representations of sentences "from the top down." It included a mechanism for transfer of semantic features from one constituent to another in cases like the ones just discussed. For example, the feature *female* would be transferred from "pretty" to some noun it modified, such as "neighbor."

As a result of continuing work on semantics and on syntax, in the mid-1960's a new conception of linguistic structure emerged, a conception most fully described in two books: *An Integrated Theory of Linguistic Descriptions* (Katz and Postal 1964) and *Aspects of the Theory of Syntax* (Chomsky 1965). The new model dispensed with the notion of "kernel sentence" as being linguistically unimportant, drawing instead a distinction between the *deep structures* and the *surface structures* of all sentences. The surface structures are the grammatical forms of sentences as they are actually spoken; the deep structures are abstract underlying forms which must be postulated in order to account fully for linguistic regularities. It was discovered in a significant number of cases that the deep structures which had to be postulated on syntactic grounds turned out to contain information which was crucial to semantic interpretation, and which was missing from the surface structures. To take an example which has become familiar, there is a restriction that reflexive objects in imperative sentences must be in the second person—it's all right to say "Go wash yourself!", but not "*Go wash himself!''. The simplest way to explain this is to assume that imperative sentences are actually surface realizations of underlying forms containing a second person subject (something like "You will go wash yourself!"). Then the rule governing the appearance of reflexive pronouns applies in its regular way to the underlying form of imperatives before the rule of imperative formation deletes the "you." But now notice that an important aspect of the semantics of imperative sentences is that they are understood as addressed to the second person. This is what lies behind the traditional grammatical assertion that the subject of an imperative sentence is "you understood." According to the analysis just proposed, imperative sentences have "you" as the subject of their underlying or deep structures, although it is not present in the surface sentence. Thus if semantic interpretation is interpretation of deep structures, one otherwise puzzling aspect of the semantics of imperative sentences is explained.

Katz and Postal pushed this model to its logical extreme, arguing that syntactic deep structures contain all of the information required for semantic interpretation of a sentence, and the transformations which apply to derive surface structures from them add nothing to the meaning. They offered a number of arguments to show that transformations which had previously been thought to cause a semantic change, such as the rule for question formation, in fact depend for their applicability on the presence of certain triggering elements or configurations in the deep structure, and that the semantic "load" thought to be carried by the transformation in fact resides in the trigger. Thus Katz and Postal's projection rules interpreted syntactic deep structures only.

Independent work in phonology (the study of sound systems of languages) had already pretty conclusively demonstrated that phonological rules require information about surface syntactic structures, and can be said to be "interpretive" in the same sense that semantics was said to be interpretive above. A very pleasing picture thus emerged—a tripartite model of language consisting of a syntactic component which is generative (that is, responsible for the infinity of language, and logically basic) and semantic and phonological components which are interpretive. The semantic component interprets the syntactic deep structures, and the phonological component interprets the syntactic surface structures. This was the "integrated" theory of Katz and Postal's title, and it was accepted and elaborated upon by Chomsky in *Aspects*.

This conception of the relationship between syntax and semantics has come increasingly under attack in the last two or three years. Many linguists now feel that the notion of deep structure as syntactically generated and semantically interpreted is untenable. They do not deny that sentences have abstract underlying structures, but they conceive of these structures as the semantic representations proper of the sentences, with no intervening level between semantic representation and surface structure which can be defined in purely syntactic, nonsemantic terms. Other linguists have tried to show instances of transformational rules which have an effect on meaning. These questions are still highly controversial, and their resolution is among the linguistic tasks of the immediate future.

In the study of lexicon, or vocabulary structure, the most important single development has been the concept that vocabulary items, or morphemes, are not simple atomic entities semantically, but rather have complex internal structures. Thus for example "father" is analyzable as *male parent*, "uncle" as *parent's male sibling*, and "aunt" as *parent's female sibling*. Such an analysis provides a natural way of representing the similarities and differences among the terms analyzed, which was set forth earlier as one of the empirical goals of linguistic semantics. "Father" and "uncle" are similar in that both are *male*, while "aunt" and "uncle" are similar in that both are *parent's sibling*. Meaning components like *male* and *sibling* are called **semantic features**.

The determination of the feature composition of morphemes is called **componential analysis**. Componential analysis was first developed by anthropological linguists to describe terminological systems of various languages which were of interest in cultural anthropology, e.g. color terms and kinship terms. An excellent example of componential analysis and a bibliography are contained in (Lounsbury 1962).

Semantic features are abstractions postulated to explain certain linguistic phenomena, just as the deep syntactic structures already discussed. The phenomena they account for are first of all intuitive judgments of similarity or difference of vocabulary items by native speakers. It has long been a controversial question in linguistics, however, whether intuitive judgments offer a sufficiently objective basis for scientific analysis. There has therefore been a continuing search for independent justification of particular semantic features postulated in componential analysis.

In the article already referred to, Lounsbury analyzed the system of kinship terms of the Seneca Indians. He showed three different possible analyses, utilizing three different (but overlapping) sets of semantic features. He then showed that according to traditional linguistic methodological principles, used extensively in phonological analysis, one of these three solutions is clearly simpler and more general than the other two, and therefore to be preferred. Unfortunately, Lounsbury's elegant and very convincing arguments are applicable only in highly structured vocabulary domains such as the one he was studying, where it is possible to place the forms into a complete and unexceptionable paradigm, and where the distinctions among the forms are clear. The more usual situation is that there is a confusing welter of ways to organize the data, and any particular organization proposed may be objected to as arbitrary in the absence of independent justification.

Katz and Fodor's theory of lexical structure was somewhat richer than a simple "bundle-of-features" model, the extra machinery being occasioned by the needs of the semantic theory of which it was a part. Recall that the basic operation of semantic interpretation in Katz and Fodor's framework is an amalgamation of the features of lower-level constituents into a feature complex for the higher-level constituents which they comprise, with elimination of incompatible sets of features. The specification of incompatibilities to be eliminated is accomplished by what Katz and Fodor call **selection restrictions**. These are different from ordinary semantic features in that they don't specify semantic properties of a vocabulary item itself, but rather semantic properties which some other item must have in order to be compatible with it. Thus *human* and *female* are properties of "woman," but *female* is not a property of "pregnant" as such; rather it is a necessary property of any noun modified by "pregnant" (silences and pauses excepted). An announcement that "Mildred's favorite actor is pregnant" makes you uncomfortable because "actor" has the semantic property *male*, which violates the selection restriction on "pregnant." Now given the existence of these sorts of selectional incompatibilities, and the mechanism of selection restrictions to account for them, Katz and Fodor have a way of justifying the features they propose as inherent semantic properties of lexical items: a semantic feature is to be postulated if and only if it plays a role in some selection restriction. Thus given the English word "pregnant," with the sort of selection restriction just described, we are justified in postulating *female* as a semantic feature active in English.

There are two problems with this approach. First of all, for any single vocabulary item there is virtually an unlimited number of contexts in which it will be anomalous. This point was made forcefully by Bolinger (1965); Bolinger's argument takes a different form, but the point is the same. Take "dog," for example. "My dog flew up into the tree" is odd; *wingless* must be a property of "dog." "My dog is left-handed"; here the peculiarity has to do not only with the absence of hands, but also with the lack, in dogs, of a type of asymmetry we find in people, sugars, and scissors. The oddness of "My dog overshadowed our house" and "My dog fell into an envelope" means that the relative sizes of houses and dogs, and of dogs and envelopes, must be marked in the dictionary entry for "dog." Such observations would appear to render hopeless at the outset the serious application of Katz and Fodor's proposed principle for justifying the postulation of particular semantic features.

The second problem is that there are certain groups of words which are semantically distinct from each other but which don't differ in terms of selection restrictions. Color terms are a good example—wherever "red" can be used, "green" can be used with no higher degree of semantic anomaly, although of course the use of one might be factually more correct than the other. That is to say, sentences like "Grass is red" or "Stop signs are green" are factually wrong, but not semantically peculiar in the sense of the examples we've been discussing. To know that they are wrong, we need some extralinguistic information about the world. But if there is no difference in their selection restrictions, how to account for the clear semantic difference between "green" and "red"?

Katz and Fodor recognized this difficulty, and to meet it proposed a further enrichment of the semantic structure of lexical items. Besides semantic features (*semantic markers*, in Katz and Fodor's term) and selection restrictions, they proposed that each lexical item has a *distinguisher*. The distinguisher indicates just those aspects of the semantic content of the term which are "idiosyncratic," i.e., which distinguish that term from other terms but which do not otherwise enter into the semantic system of the language. In particular, the semantic aspects indicated by distinguishers do not enter into selection restrictions. Thus all of the color terms of a language would have a common set of semantic markers and selection restrictions, which we can abbreviate as COLOR, and then each individual color term would be distinguished from the rest by a distinguisher, which can be represented as a numerical subscript on COLOR. So "green" might be $COLOR_4$, "red" $COLOR_7$, "purple" $COLOR_{12}$, and so on.

Two criticisms can be made of this move. First, it constitutes merely a recognition of the problem, and not progress toward a solution. Distinguishers are in fact a catch-all category for those aspects of the semantic content of lexical items not amenable to investigation by the fundamental technique. They have no inherent defining properties. Second, in many cases the distinguisher approach, as outlined above for color terms, is clearly understructured. Lounsbury's analysis of kinship terms, already mentioned, is a case in point. The kinship terms of any language form a cohesive domain, like color terms, with no difference in selection restrictions among the various terms. Thus following Katz and Fodor's model, they must be differentiated by distinguishers. But as Lounsbury's analysis clearly shows, merely to distinguish them is to fail to say all that can be said about them; the domain has a rich internal structure of great linguistic interest.

Another approach to validating the postulation of semantic features of vocabulary items was taken by Bendix (1966), a student of Weinreich's. Bendix' method was reminiscent of certain kinds of research in the social sciences. He worked with groups of informants, native speakers of English, Hindi, and Japanese, giving them open-ended and forced-choice interpretation tests and relative acceptability tests of sentences containing the verbs he was interested in analyzing. These were all verbs or verb-like constructions involving the notion of "having" in their semantic interpretations. In English, the verbs were "get," "find," "give," "lend," "borrow," "take," "get rid of," "lose," and "keep." He then tabulated the responses, and whenever the bulk of his informants agreed on a response (which was usually the case, because of the way the tests were constructed) he took that as empirical validation of the aspect of the analysis being tested.

The open-ended test which Bendix used for exploratory purposes consisted of asking informants to interpret a sentence in which two of the verbs to be analyzed are placed in contrasting positions, e.g. "He didn't give it to me, he lent it to me." "By this means," writes Bendix, "we hope to identify the components that mark the paradigmatic oppositions between the meanings in the system." (1966, p. 18) This test was followed by tests in which the range of possible responses was drastically narrowed, for testing particular semantic features which were postulated as a result of the first test. There were several of these, all similar in that they required the informant to make a choice as to which of a pair of sentences made more sense. Some examples:

Since he's only lent it to me, $\left\{\begin{array}{l}\text{it's}\\ \text{it isn't}\end{array}\right\}$ really mine.

He's lost his watch, but he $\left\{\begin{array}{l}\text{knows}\\ \text{doesn't know}\end{array}\right\}$ where it is.

On the basis of a series of such tests, Bendix devised a paradigm of marked shared features of the verbs under analysis. Features used in the paradigm include such things as *A has B after a particular time* (true, for example, of "A finds B," and of "C gives A B," but false for "A loses B"), and *chance causes the occurrence* (true of "A loses B," but false for "A gets rid of B").

The criticism to be made here is that a great deal of machinery has been set up to no particular avail. A native speaker of the language under analysis is required to formulate the tests, and that same native speaker would be able to predict the results with unfailing accuracy. Since the tests can never yield a surprising result, they are of questionable value. Those who seek an independent justification for features postulated in componential analysis should not be satisfied with questionnaire procedures like those employed by Bendix. An intuitive judgment made by any number of people is still an intuitive judgment.

Recent, still unpublished work by the author and others (Chapin 1971) has indicated the possible usefulness of an approach to componential analysis based on mapping particular vocabulary domains from one language to another. Except in a restricted class of cases (roughly, nouns naming objects which can be pointed out, such as yams, horses, and mountains) the vocabularies of even very closely related languages do not match each other exactly; that is, a single word in one language may have three or four different translations in the other language, depending on the context and on the exact sense intended. The hypothesis which motivates this line of research is that the differences in the "sense intended" correspond to semantic features which are specified in the language with the three or four words but neutralized in the language with one serving for all. For example, the English preposition "across" can introduce a prepositional phrase which can describe the location of a stationary object, as in "The Post Office is across the street," or the route of a moving object, as in "Florence swam across the English Channel." A linguist analyzing English prepositions would notice this semantic variability of "across," but without reference to other languages he would have only his intuitions to rely on in postulating a feature to account for it, a feature neutralized in "across." If he examines the Russian prepositional system, however, comparing it to the English, he discovers that the former sense of "across" translates into Russian *za*, and the latter sense as *cherez*. This difference in translation justifies the postulation of a feature distinguishing the two senses. Conversely, a linguist studying Russian alone might have an intuition that *za* and *cherez* are semantically related; his discovery that these two prepositions receive the same English translation would be an independent confirmation of this intuition.

It is still too early to assess the value of this approach. Research must continue. The encouraging prospect is that there is growing agreement on the empirical goals of linguistic semantics, the right questions to ask. Progress has been slow in the past because people have not really been working on the same problems. Thus it has been impossible for one person to build on the work of another, and even impossible to make coherent criticisms of another's work. If agreement is being reached as to the interesting questions, that is the greatest achievement of linguistic semantics today.

Acknowledgments

This essay is one result of research initiated while I was a Fellow of the Humanities Institute of the University of California. I am grateful to the Institute for its support. I would also like to acknowledge the many helpful suggestions made by Susan Chapin, Stanley Chodorow, Roderick Jacobs, and Ronald Langacker.

Bibliography

BENDIX, E. *Componential Analysis of General Vocabulary,* Publication 41 of the Indiana University Research Center in Anthropology, Folklore, and Linguistics. Published as a supplement to *International Journal of American Linguistics,* Vol. 32, No. 2 (1966).

BLOOMFIELD, L. *Language,* New York: Holt, Rinehart & Winston, 1933.

BOLINGER, D. "The Atomization of Meaning," *Language,* Vol. 41, No. 4 (1965), pp. 555–573.

CHAPIN, P. "What's in a Word?: Some Considerations in Lexicological Theory," *Papers in Linguistics,* Vol. 4 (1971).

CHOMSKY, N. *Syntactic Structures,* The Hague: Mouton, 1957.

————. *Aspects of the Theory of Syntax,* Cambridge, Mass.: M.I.T. Press, 1965.

KATZ, J., and J. FODOR. "The Structure of a Semantic Theory," *Language,* Vol. 39, No. 2 (1963), pp. 170–210. Reprinted in Fodor and Katz (eds.), *The Structure of Language,* Englewood Cliffs, N.J.: Prentice-Hall, 1964, pp. 479–518.

————, and P. POSTAL. *An Integrated Theory of Linguistic Descriptions,* Cambridge, Mass.: M.I.T. Press, 1964.

LOUNSBURY, F. "Structural Analysis of Kinship Semantics," in Lunt (ed.), *Proceedings of the IXth International Congress of Linguists,* The Hague: Mouton, 1962, pp. 1073–1090.

WEINREICH, U. "On the Semantic Structure of Language," in Greenberg (ed.), *Universals of Language,* Cambridge, Mass.: The M.I.T. Press, 1963, pp. 114–171. For purposes of assigning historical priority, it should be noted that although this publication did not appear in print until 1963, it was originally prepared for a conference held in April 1961.

————. "Explorations in Semantic Theory," in Sebeok (ed.), *Current Trends in Linguistics 3: Theoretical Foundations,* The Hague: Mouton, 1966, pp. 395–477.

Voici and *Voilà*

Bernard Tranel

In traditional grammars of French, *voici* and *voilà* (sometimes translated "here is/are" and "there is/are" respectively) have a very indefinite status. Within the same grammar, they have been assigned to different parts of speech. I would first like to show that these words should be in fact considered as verbal elements.

Most of the time, *voici* and *voilà* are considered as adverbs and/or prepositions. Such an analysis is based on a very superficial consideration of surface structures. For instance, Grévisse (1969, p. 131) classifies *voici* and *voilà* as adverbs because of the parallelism between (1) and (2):

    (1) Assurément que vous avez raison.
        (You are definitely right.)
    (2) Voilà que nous sommes fâchés maintenant.
        (There, we are angry at each other now.)[1]

Immediately, restrictions on the distribution of *voici* and *voilà* can be observed, which show that *voici* and *voilà* should not be regarded as adverbs. Consider for instance (3), which is grammatical, and (4), which is not:

    (3) Vous avez assurément raison.
        (You are definitely right.)
    (4) *Nous sommes voilà fâchés maintenant.

---

[1] Most of the translations given for *voici* and *voilà* sentences are approximate, due to the very particular usage of these terms.

In spite of the fact that *voici* and *voilà* are also often listed (e.g. Grévisse, 1969, p. 890) as prepositions, there are no examples where genuine prepositions and *voici* and *voilà* seem to alternate in some kind of parallel structures.

Actually, there is a fair amount of evidence in favor of considering *voici* and *voilà* as verbal elements.

1. In most dialects, *voici* and *voilà* occur in interrogative sentences and are then constructed *est-ce que* or *-t-il*, in the same way as ordinary verbs:

    (5) Est-ce que ne voilà pas de la pourpre? (Hugo, *L'homme qui rit*)
       (Isn't that purple?)
    (6) Est-ce qu'il ne parle pas anglais?
       (Doesn't he speak English?)
    (7) Ne voilà-t-il pas une tragédie qui a bien rempli son objet? (Rousseau, *Lettre à d'Alembert*)
       (Isn't that a tragedy which accomplished its purpose?)
    (8) Ne parle-t-il pas anglais?
       (Doesn't he speak English?)

2. *Voici* and *voilà* may also occur in negative sentences, and in such constructions the negation *ne . . . pas* surrounds *voici* and *voilà* in the same way in which it surrounds verbs when they are not in the infinitive:

    (9) Ne voilà-t-il pas ton père?
       (Isn't that your father?)
    (10) Ne regarde-t-il pas ton père?
       (Isn't he looking at your father?)

In colloquial French, the particle *ne* is often deleted; and that happens with *voici* and *voilà* as well as with verbs:

    (11) Voilà-t-il pas monsieur qui ricane déjà? (Molière, *Tartuffe*)
       (Isn't he sneering already?)
    (12) Regarde-t-il pas ton père?
       (Isn't he looking at your father?)

3. Another argument in favor of considering *voici* and *voilà* as verbal elements is the existence of *revoici* and *revoilà*, which mean *voici/voilà de nouveau* ("again"). These constructions are identical

to pairs such as *faire/refaire* ("do, redo"), *commencer/recommencer* ("begin, begin again"). This morphological process—*re*-prefixation —is characteristic of verbs and certainly not of adverbs or prepositions.

4. *Voici* and *voilà* also take complement clauses, like verbs. They may govern clauses introduced by *que*:

> (13) Voilà qu'il est une heure.
>   (It's one o'clock!)
> (14) Je vous rappelle qu'il est une heure.
>   (I am reminding you that it's one o'clock.)

They may govern an infinitival clause:

> (15) Voici venir l'orage.[2]
>   (Here's the storm coming.)
> (16) J'entends venir l'orage.
>   (I hear the storm coming.)

5. *Voici* and *voilà* obey the same rule as ordinary verbs for pronoun placement:

> (18) Le prêtre confessa l'enfant.
>   (The priest gave confession to the child.)
> (19) Le prêtre le confessa.
>   (The priest gave him confession.)
> (20) Voici Jean.
>   (Here's John.)
> (21) Le voici.
>   (Here he is.)

Object pronouns are preposed in both cases.

In view of these arguments, it seems fairly convincing that *voici* and *voilà* should be treated as verbs rather than adverbs and/or prepositions. Although they have a number of idosyncrasies, they still have numerous properties which relate them to verbs more

---

[2]It is noticeable that this last construction is extremely restricted: *venir* appears to be one of very few verbs allowing it with *voici* and *voilà*. Also the relative order of *venir* and the subject NP is inflexible:

> (17) *Voici l'orage venir.

than any other parts of speech, and it would be missing a generalization not to consider them as verbal elements.

Another common assumption made about *voici* and *voilá* is to regard them as verbs in the imperative. The reason for such an analysis is due to some of the surface peculiarities of *voici* and *voilà*: contrary to other verbs, which can usually be conjugated for mode, tense, person, and number, *voici* and *voilà* cannot; they are invariable forms and in addition they have no overt subject. The following points, however, militate against such an interpretation.

1. Let us first look at pronoun placement for the imperative. The rule for preposing object pronouns does not apply:

(22) Regardez Pierre.
     (Look at Peter.)
(23) Regardez-le.
     (Look at him.)
(24) *Le regardez.

But as we have already seen, it applies with *voici* and *voilà*:

(25) Voici Pierre.
(26) *Voici-le.
(27) Le voici.

2. Secondly, *voici* and *voilà* can occur in relative clauses, which is not the case for imperatives:

(28) La jeune fille que voici est aveugle.
     (The girl here is blind.)
(29) *La jeune fille que regardez est aveugle.
     (*The girl that look is blind.)

3. A third point is that semantically, *voici* and *voilà* obviously do not express anything like an order or a wish. They merely "indicate," "point out." In this sense, they have been correctly described by traditional grammarians as *présentatifs* (Grévisse, 1969, p. 890).

I would now like to try and derive *voici* and *voilà* in a way similar to Postal's treatment of the verb *remind*. (Postal, 1970). The goal of the proposed analysis is to explain some of the characteristics of those verbal elements in terms of the combination of properties which pertain to other verbs and which are more general than the surface idiosyncrasies of *voici* and *voilà*.

In many languages, verbs of perception behave somewhat differently from other verbs. They allow constructions which are unique to the semantic class that they form. In French, they allow object nouns with a non-restrictive relative clause. Consider for instance (30) and (31):

> (30) J'entends Jean qui vient.
> (I hear John coming.)
> (31) Je vois Jean qui crie.
> (I see John shouting.)

as opposed to (32) and (33):

> (32) *J'ai blessé Jean qui vient.
> (*I hurt John coming.)
> (33) *J'attends Pierre qui crie.
> (*I wait for Peter shouting.)

Voici and *voilà* take the same construction as *entendre* and *voir* in (30) and (31):

> (34) Voici Jean qui vient.
> (Here's John coming.)
> (35) Voilà Jean qui crie.
> (There's John shouting.)

This kind of construction being restricted to a particular semantic class, it seems that we would miss a generalization if we did not somehow relate *voici* and *voilà* to verbs of perception like *entendre* and *voir*.

To this effect, an abstract verb of perception can be postulated as part of the semantic representation of *voici* and *voilà*. In fact, such a verb is not only justified on syntactic grounds; it is also needed from a semantic point of view. Every time a speaker uses *voici* or *voilà*, it is assumed that perception, in one form or another, is involved. Consider, for example, a man deprived of all five of his senses, who could still talk, and who would say (36):

> (36) Voilà Jean qui pleure.
> (There's John weeping.)

The immediate reaction of the listeners would be one of surprise. They would think that the man was extraordinary indeed, a man endowed with a sixth sense. So, whether it is regular perception or extra-sensory perception, some kind of perception is implied in *voici* and *voilà*. Marginally, we may notice some historical corroboration: *voici* and *voilà* are indeed derived from the verb *voir* (Grévisse, 1969, p. 583). An abstract verb of perception as part of the semantic representation of *voici* and *voilà* is therefore justified on both syntactic and semantic grounds.

Turning to negative and interrogative sentences with *voici* and *voilà*, we can observe interesting restrictions. Let us first examine the case of negation in declarative sentences. Consider the following two groups of sentences:

(37) *Ne voilà pas l'enfant.
(There isn't the child.)
(38) Voilà l'enfant.
(There is the child.)
(39) *Ne le voilà plus.
(There he is no longer.)
(40) Le voilà.
(There he is.)
(41) *Ne voilà jamais son livre.
(*There's his book never.)
(42) Voilà son livre.
(There's his book.)

But:

(43) Ne le voilà guère bavard maintenant.
(He's not very talkative now.)
(44) Le voilà bavard maintenant.
(He is talking now.)
(45) Ne voilà que trois ans qu'il prépare le même examen.
(It's only three years that he's been preparing for the same examination.)
(46) Voilà trois ans qu'il prépare le même examen.
(For three years he's been preparing for the same examination.)

It seems that in some cases, *voici* and *voilà* can take the negation, but not in others. The difference lies in the scope of the negations.

Ne . . . guère ("hardly") and *ne . . . que* ("only") in fact modify *bavard* and *trois ans* respectively, and not *voilà*; they are not true negations; (43) and (45) can actually be paraphrased as (47) and (48):

(47) Le voilà peu bavard maintenant.
(He's not very talkative now.)

(48) Voilà seulement trois ans qu'il prépare le même examen.
(It's only three years that he has been preparing for the same examination.)

where obviously *peu* modifies *bavard* and *seulement* modifies *trois ans*. On the other hand, the scope of *ne . . . pas* ("not"), *ne . . . plus* ("not any more"), and *ne . . . jamais* ("never") in (37), (39), and (41) is the verb itself.

(49) is an interesting sentence because of its ambiguity:

(49) Ne voilà pas trois ans qu'il prépare cet examen.

The sentence will be grammatical or ungrammatical depending on what part of the sentence the negation applies to. If the negation modifies *trois ans*, the sentence is grammatical and can be paraphrased as (50):

(50) Voilà à peine trois ans qu'il prépare cet examen.
(It's hardly three years that he has been preparing for that examination.)

If the scope of the negation is *voilà*, then the sentence is ungrammatical, just as (37) was.

We can therefore say that *voici* and *voilà* cannot be negated in declarative sentences.

Looking now at interrogative sentences with *voici* and *voilà*, we can notice that unless *voici* or *voilà* are negated, the sentences are ungrammatical:

(51) *Voilà-t-il ton père?
(Is that your father?)

(52) Ne voilà-t-il pas ton père?
(Isn't that your father?)

Furthermore, the negation has to be *ne . . . pas*. Other negations associated with *voici* or *voilà* produce ungrammatical sentences:

(53) *Ne voici-t-il plus ton père?
(54) *Ne voilà-t-il jamais son livre?
(55) *Ne le voilà-t-il guère bavard?
(56) *Ne voilà-t-il que trois ans qu'il prépare le même examen?

In (55) and (56), the negations do not modify *voilà*, as was the case in the corresponding declarative sentences (43) and (45). (55) and (56) can therefore be assumed to belong to the same class of ungrammatical sentences as (51).

We are thus left with three problems: (a) the ungrammaticality of negative declarative sentences, (b) the ungrammaticality of non-negated interrogative sentences, (c) the grammaticality of interrogative sentences with *ne . . . pas*. These restrictions on the use of *voici* and *voilà* are intuitively felt to be related and they should therefore be accounted for in the same way. In order to try and explain those restrictions, the semantics of *voici* and *voilà* should be examined more closely.

It has been noted already that *voici* and *voilà* "indicate" or "point out," that they are *présentatifs*. In other words, the speaker performs an act—the act of indicating—by saying *voici* or *voilà*. Semantically, it is therefore reasonable to postulate a performative verb of indication as part of the meaning of *voici* and *voilà*, for example something like "I point out to you that. . . ." The semantic representation of *voici* and *voilà* would thus be composed of a performative verb of indication and a verb of perception.

This combination, which is semantically well-motivated, also explains the syntactic restrictions that were observed.

Let us first examine the case of the negation. Conceivably, in a sentence like (57):

(57) *Ne voila pas que Jean prépare son examen.

the negation NEG could originate in three places: its scope could be the lowest sentence or the verb of perception or the performative verb. If NEG had originated in the lowest sentence, a possible surface structure would have been (58):

(58) Voilà que Jean ne prépare pas son examen.
     So John is not preparing for his examination.

and (57) would come from (58) by NEG-raising. But (57) is not grammatical, whereas (58) is. This can be explained by the fact that verbs of perception are factive verbs, and we know independently that factive verbs do not allow NEG-raising.[3]

If the scope of NEG had been the verb of perception, then there would have been no perception involved, which is contrary to our intuition about *voici* and *voilà*. More formally, the semantic tree structure would not have satisfied the structural description of the lexical transformation inserting *voici* and *voilà*, the reason being the presence of NEG between the performative verb and the verb of perception.

If the scope of NEG had been the performative verb itself (i.e. "I do NOT indicate to you that . . ."), the performative verb would have lost its property of being a performative, and the lexical insertion rule would have been blocked again, because the lexical insertion of *voici* and *voilà* requires a performative verb in the semantic tree structure.

For questions without negations, identical arguments apply to prevent the derivations from surfacing. If the performative verb is questioned or if the question applies to the verb of perception, the lexical insertion rule cannot take place.

There remains to explain why a negative interrogative sentence with *ne . . . pas* is grammatical, where apparently there would be two sets of reasons why it should not be grammatical, and why the same does not apply to interrogative sentences with other negations.

Consider (59) and (60):

(59) Ne voilà-t-il pas que Jean porte un pull-over rouge? (Isn't John wearing a red pullover?)

---

[3] The verb *realize*, unlike the verb *suppose*, is a factive verb. Compare

    (a) I realized that Joseph was not coming.
    (b) I supposed that Joseph was not coming.

Sentence (a), but not sentence (b), presupposes that the speaker accepts it as a fact that Joseph was not coming. Interestingly it is possible to raise the negative-element into the next higher clause, *if the verb in that clause is a non-factive verb*, without changing the basic meaning. Thus (d) is basically synonymous with (b), but (c) is not basically synonymous with (a):

    (c) I didn't realize that Joseph was coming.
    (d) I didn't suppose that Joseph was coming.

(See Kiparsky and Kiparsky, 1970).

(60) *Ne voilà-t-il plus que Jean porte un pull-over rouge?
(Isn't John wearing a red pullover any longer?)

It appears that whereas negation and question each individually block any sentence with *voici* or *voilà*, those blocking properties cancel out when they occur in the same sentence, and when NEG = *ne . . . pas*.

In fact, this is not surprising if we examine the semantics of (59) and (60) more closely. As opposed to (51), (59) is not a true question: this is because of the presence of *ne . . . pas*; rather, it is a rhetorical question—or some kind of strong exclamation—where the speaker actually means the affirmative of the proposition that is questioned and negated on the surface. Thus, uttering (59) is equivalent to saying (61):

(61) Voilà que Jean porte un pull-over rouge.
(There's John wearing a red pullover.)

Although (60) presumably is a rhetorical question too, its declarative equivalent (62)

(62) *Ne voilà plus que Jean porte un pull-over rouge.
(There's John no longer wearing a red pullover.)

is not an affirmative sentence, but a negative one, and we have seen that such sentences are ungrammatical.

The difference in grammaticality between (59) and (60) is thus explained by reducing them to the more basic sentences of which they seem to be surface versions.

After showing that *voici* and *voilà* are best considered as verbal elements, I have atomized them into two abstract verbs, a performative verb of indication and a verb of perception. The combination of those two verbs provides the right semantic representation for *voici* and *voilà*. In addition, the main syntactic properties of the two constituent verbs merge to account for some of the most striking idiosyncrasies of *voici* and *voilà*.

This analysis has also shown that performative verbs do not necessarily occur as the highest verbs in a sentence (as is claimed by Ross, 1970) since *voici* and *voilà* may be embedded in relative clauses, and that they are not always deletable, but that they may form part of the meaning of another verb, in the present case in alliance with a verb of perception.

Bibliography

GRÉVISSE, MAURICE. *Le Bon Usage*. Gembloux, Belgium: Duculot, and Paris: Hatier, 1969.

KIPARSKY, PAUL and KIPARSKY, CAROL. "Fact" in Bierwisch and Heidolph (eds.), *Progress in Linguistics*. The Hague: Mouton and Co., 1970.

POSTAL, PAUL M. "On the Surface Verb 'Remind'" in *Linguistic Inquiry*, Vol. 1, No. 1 (1970).

ROSS, J. R. "On Declarative Sentences" in Jacobs and Rosenbaum (eds.), *Readings in English Transformational Grammar* (Lexington, Mass.: Xerox College Publishing, 1970.

Some Remarks on Adverbs

S.-Y. Kuroda

1. In English, adverbs may be formed by adding the suffix *-ly* to adjectives. For example, *elegant*, *reluctant*, *probable*, *unbelievable* and *extraordinary* are adjectives, and *elegantly*, *reluctantly*, *probably*, *unbelievably* and *extraordinarily* are adverbs obtained by adding *-ly* to these adjectives.

Adverbs thus obtained from adjectives have different functions depending on the source adjectives. The adverbs *elegantly* and *reluctantly* in the following sentences are examples of so-called "manner adverbs":

(1) Mary danced elegantly.
(2) Mary danced reluctantly.

Adverbs like *probably* and *unbelievably* in the following sentences are so-called "sentence adverbs":

(3) Probably, Many danced.
(4) Unbelievably, Mary danced.

Adverbs may modify adjectives as in:[1]

(5) Mary is extraordinarily beautiful.

2. Semantically, adjectives are typically words that express properties of concrete things and abstract ideas. These adjectives

---

SOURCE: Reprinted by permission of the author from *The English Record*, April 1970.

[1]This does not mean that all the different kinds of functions of adverbs formed from adjectives by means of *-ly* are exhausted here. See section 10.

may be used in a copular sentence to show that a thing or idea, the subject of the sentence, possesses a particular quality, for example,

(6) This apple is red.

This is a primary form of "predicative judgment." The adjective is said to be used predicatively in sentences like this.

On the other hand, the adjective is said to be used "attributively" when it precedes a noun and modifies it, as in:

(7) Red apples.

In transformational grammar, adjectives used attributively are related to relative clauses in which the same adjectives are used predicatively. More exactly, (7) is said to be derived from

(8) Apples which are red.

or (8) is said to be an underlying form of (7). (7) is considered to be a surface appearance of the more basic entity, (8), which represents more faithfully the semantic structure of the synonymous form (7). Semantically, (8) would imply that its meaning consists of recognition of certain objects—apples—and a predicative judgment about the perceived objects, that is

(9) These apples are red.

3. Let us here digress from our main topic in order to prevent possible misunderstanding of the contention that expressions like (8) are more basic than those like (7) in the sense of generative transformational theory. This contention is logically independent of whether or not attributive expressions like (7) are more primitive than expressions like (8) and/or predicative judgments like (9), which is meant to underlie (7) and (8), more primitive in the particular sense that the former are learned earlier in the process of language learning than the latter. In fact, from the theory of transformational grammar as such, no conclusion may be drawn as to whether or not generative grammar is learned from more basic forms, in the technical sense, progressing to more derived forms—more derived in the sense that their generation needs more formal machinery. To put it another way, in their search for base forms in the technical sense of generative grammar, linguists must neither be restrained, nor guided, by empirical evidence as to what forms are learned at what stages of learning.

In our present case, it would be quite possible that children learn attributive expressions like (7) first, before they acquire expressions for the primary type of predicative judgment illustrated by (9); it is quite implausible that they use forms like (8) before they use forms like (7). It is a separate psychological question—assuming that children first acquire attributive expressions like (7)—whether or not children at this stage must be assumed to be capable of making, in some way or other, the primary type of predicative judgment expressed by forms like (9) in adult language. But, at any rate, in the process of language learning, after a while they acquire the expression of the primary predicative judgment like (9) and more general types of predicative judgments that are expressed by noncopular sentences like:

(10) Those dogs don't bark.

Furthermore, they proceed to learn how to construct complex notions, of which

(11) Dogs that don't bark

would be a general type of example. But they would immediately realize that this procedure can also be applied to sentences like (9) to obtain forms like (8). At this stage, they would acquire the knowledge that (7) and (8) are synonymous and these two forms would be related in their grammar. Then, since a general pattern of formation of complex notions has now been acquired and is represented in the forms illustrated by (8) and (11), the semantic understanding of forms like (7) would be subsumed according to this general pattern, and would remain only as a particular syntactic realization of a special case of this one general semantic schema.[2]

---

[2]To avoid confusion, it must be noted that by the attributive use of an adjective is meant here the attributive use in the proper sense, and not in all instances of the prenominal use of so-called adjectives. Actually, it is not so easy a task to give, syntactically and/or semantically, an exact definition of the attributive use of an adjective in the proper sense. Here we must be content with a brief and tentative definition of the proper attributive use of an adjective, with some examples of the prenominal use of adjectives that are not attributive in the proper sense. Formally, one may say that an adjective used prenominally is properly attributive if it can be paraphrased by a relative clause in which the adjective is used predicatively. (The contention in section 2 is not merely a repetition of this definition, since the former

4. Let us now go back to our adverbs, *elegantly*, *reluctantly*, *probably*, *unbelievably* and *extraordinarily*. So far as morphology is concerned, one can simply say that these adverbs are derived from the corresponding adjectives by adding the suffix *-ly*. But just how is this relevant semantically? Does this morphologic process correspond to some primitive semantic process by means of which adjectival concepts are converted into certain different units of thought?

It has been noted before that the so-called attributive use of an adjective is reduced to the so-called predicative use. Should it not also be the case that the adverbial use of an adjective with the suffix *-ly* must also be reduced to the predicative use?

We shall deal with different uses of adverbs case by case.

5. Let us first consider sentence adverbs like *probably* and *unbelievably*. What would be the subjects of predicative judgments, if any, that assign them attributes of *probability* and *unbelievability*, and that are semantically involved in the propositions represented by (3) and (4) (which we repeat here)?

(3) Probably, Mary danced.
(4) Unbelievably, Mary danced.

To put it briefly, what is *probable*, and what is *unbelievable*? *That Mary danced.*

In fact, (3) and (4) may be paraphrased by

(12) That Mary danced is probable.

and

(13) That Mary danced is unbelievable.

---

claims that the predicative use is basic in the generative sense.) Semantically, an adjective used attributively in the proper sense purports to add to the notion of the noun it modifies just the concept it represents when it is used predicatively. Thus *red* in *red wine* (as opposed to *white wine*) is not properly attributive; red wine is indeed red, but the notion of red wine does not simply consist of wineness and redness, but also of whatever flavor or taste that distinguishes it from white wine. A celebrated example, *criminal lawyer*, in the sense of a lawyer who specializes in criminal law, illustrates another type of the improper attributive use of an adjective; criminal lawyers are not necessarily, or perhaps very rarely, criminal. One can distinguish many different types of the improper attributive use of adjectives; syntactic and semantic problems related to their nature and origin are diverse, difficult, and sometimes quite subtle.

respectively. More common equivalents to these would be:

(14) It is probable that Mary danced.

and

(15) It is unbelievable that Mary danced.

To put it simply, and hence not quite exactly, the transformational linguist assumes that sentences like (14) and (15) are derived from those like (12) and (13). It is not a matter of recent development, on the other hand, that, on an informal basis, sentences like (3) and (4) are related to sentences like (14) and (15). In terms of transformational grammar, (12) and (13) are assumed to be the base forms of (3) and (4) respectively; in these base forms the adverbs are reduced to the corresponding adjectives in the predicative use.

6. Let us now proceed to the so-called manner adverbs. It is generally said that adverbs that answer the question "How?" are manner adverbs. Thus,

(16.1) How did Mary dance?
(16.2) She danced elegantly.
(17.1) How did Mary dance?
(17.2) She danced reluctantly.

But *elegantly* and *reluctantly* represent different classes of manner adverbs. For the time being, we shall be concerned only with the manner adverbs like *elegantly* and related expressions.

Again, given (1),

(1) Mary danced elegantly.

we may ask: what is (or was) *elegant*? What predicative judgment, if any, is semantically involved in sentence (1), and what is its subject? To see the answer, it is better to try to make up a more complicated answer to question (16.1), in order that general semantic characteristics involved in the problem become apparent. Assume, for example, that seeing Mary dance elegantly, someone was reminded of Pavlova and, answering (16.1), wanted to express it. He would perhaps say

(18) Mary danced in a manner that reminded us of Pavlova.

Here, the noun *manner* is modified by a relative clause. This is the general way to convey any conceptually complicated manner of an action (or a manner that has any complicated effect). In fact, this general way of expressing manner is reduced to the general way of expressing complex notions. And, even when the manner of the action in question is conceptually relatively simple, as in (1), one could use an expression which conforms with this general pattern; instead of (1), one could say,

(19) Mary danced in a manner that was elegant.

or, according to the general rule that converts predicatively used adjectives into attributively used ones,

(20) Mary danced in an elegant manner.

While (19) is perhaps too clumsy an expression to be used in actual speech, (20) is quite an acceptable form, and it paraphrases (1). One may say, then, that the predicative judgment

(21) The manner was elegant.

is semantically involved in sentence (1).

In fact, the contention that adverbs like *elegantly* do not represent another primitive pattern of thought, but rather must be reduced to expressions like *in an elegant manner*, can be traced back at least to the seventeenth century rationalist French grammarians.[3] It was recently reproduced in the theoretical scheme of transformational grammar.[4] Thus, technically, sentences like (1) are said to be derived from sentences like (20), and hence, ultimately, from base forms like (19). Such base forms represent explicitly the claim that the semantic function of the adjectives contained in adverbs like *elegantly* is simply a predicate function.

Recently, a somewhat different syntactic analysis of sentences like (1) has been proposed.[5] According to this proposal, sentences like (1) are assumed to be derived from syntactic base forms that are

---

[3]See Chomsky, Noam. *Cartesian Linguistics.* New York, 1966, p. 42 ff.

[4]See Katz, Jerrold J. and Postal, Paul M. *An Integrated Theory of Linguistic Descriptions.* Cambridge, Mass., 1964, p. 141.

[5]See Kuroda, S.-Y. (1968), "Some remarks on English manner adverbials," to appear in *Studies in General and Oriental Linguistics,* a commemorative volume dedicated to Dr. Shiro Hattori, ed. by R. Jacobson and S. Kawamoto.

different from those of (19). We shall return to this later, in section 8. But the validity of the semantic claim just stated remains, whichever syntactic solution is to be adopted.

7. Let us now consider the adverbs like *reluctantly*. Although such adverbs answer the question "How?" and are called manner adverbs, the difference between those and adverbs like *elegantly* becomes apparent if we try to establish the base form of

(2) Mary danced reluctantly.

in the way (1) has been traced back to its presumed form (19). In fact, the form which formally corresponds to the intermediate form,

(22) Mary danced in a reluctant manner.

does not sound quite right. The unnaturalness becomes much more conspicuous if one tries to bring (22) back to its presumed base form:

(23) Mary danced in a manner that was reluctant.

Obviously, this form must be rejected, and also the attempt to account for the adverb *reluctantly* in (2) by the unjustified predicative use of the adjective in this form.

This is not unexpected. The adjective *reluctant* describes a certain state of mind and can therefore only be a predicate of a human subject. Whereas one can say

(24) Mary was reluctant.

one cannot say

(25) The manner was reluctant.

The unacceptable form (23) contains this unacceptable proposition.

Reluctance can only be attributed to a human being. But (2) involves semantically the concept of *reluctance* in some way or other. Hence, it must also involve its subject, a human being. Who? *Mary.* Semantically, then, (2) involves the predicative judgment

(26) Mary was reluctant.

Thus, in the meaning expressed by (2), *Mary* is at the same time the subject of the action of *dancing* and that of the feeling of *reluctance*. In fact, (2) may be paraphrased by the following form which is, perhaps, not a very good expression, but which contains in a more explicit form the two statements of which *Mary* is the subject:

(27) Mary was reluctant in that she (Mary) danced.

This may be abbreviated to:

(28) Mary was reluctant in dancing.

Certain more formal arguments have been made for taking forms like (27) as the base forms of sentences like (2).[6] Let us content ourselves here with the observation that sentences like (2) in which adverbs like *reluctantly* appear, have thus been related semantically to expressions like (27) in which the corresponding adjectives like *reluctant* appear in the predicative use.

8. In this section the alternative proposal for the analysis of adverbs like *elegantly*, which was mentioned at the end of section 6, will be briefly sketched.

In section 6 it was pointed out that manner adverbs like *elegantly* are paraphrased by manner adverbial phrases like *in an elegant manner*, and the latter were assumed to be the base forms of the former. However, the converse does not hold: not all phrases of the form *in + a + adjective + manner* may be replaced by the corresponding adverbial form *adjective + ly*. Take, for instance, the sentence:

(29) Mary danced in an unbelievable manner.

If the phrase *in an unbelievable manner* is replaced mechanically by *unbelievably*, one obtains

(30) Mary danced unbelievably.

But this is not a good sentence, and even if it is accepted as a sentence, it does not paraphrase (29). To be sure, *unbelievably* is an authentic adverb, but it cannot be used as a manner adverb. It can be used as a sentence adverb, and since sentence adverbs are generally put at the beginning of the sentence, (30) does not sound right, whereas

(31) Unbelievably, Mary danced.

which is the same as (4), is a good sentence.

---

[6]See Lakoff, George. "On the Nature of Syntactic Irregularity," Report No. NSF-16, the Computation Laboratory of Harvard University, 1965.

Thus the rule producing manner adverbials like *elegantly* from adverbial phrases like *in an elegant manner* would not enjoy complete generality.

Is there any alternative source for the adverb *elegantly*, in which the adverb is reduced to the predicative use of the adjective *elegant*? At this point let us recall that (2), (3), and (4) are assumed to be derived from (27), (14), and (15), respectively.

(2) Mary danced reluctantly.

(27) Mary was reluctant in that she (Mary) danced.

(3) Probably, Mary danced.

(14) It is probable that Mary danced.

(4) Unbelievably, Mary danced.

(15) It is unbelievable that Mary danced.

In these source sentences, (27), (14), and (15), the adjectives, *reluctant*, *probable*, and *unbelievable*, appear as the predicates of the main sentences. Rhetorically, one may say that in these instances the adjective in the copular main sentence is *lowered down* into a subordinate sentence, taking on adverbial form; to put it another way, the adverb is derived from the corresponding adjective used predicatively in a sentence one step *higher*.

Derivation of the adverb *elegantly* would also be covered by this pattern if, instead of (20), or ultimately (19), the sentence

(32) The manner in which Mary danced was elegant.

is assumed to be the base of (1). If the relative clause of this sentence is extraposed, resemblance of this base to those of (27), (14), and (15) would appear closer:

(33) The manner was elegant in which Mary danced.

Proposing this alternative base form for (1) does not alone suffice to clarify syntactic problems related to our topic. In fact, one can immediately see that exactly the same trouble can be pointed out concerning the new proposal as the one pointed out above for the former analysis. For as well as (32) one may have:

(34) The manner in which Mary danced was unbelievable.

whereas, as has been noted, (30) may not be obtained from this. But in this paper it is not proposed to go into detailed syntactic arguments for the base form (32) and related discussions.[7] Let us simply note that in this alternative base form (32) of (1), *elegant* appears as the predicate of *manner* as it was in the formerly proposed base form (19).

9. Let us now turn our attention to

(5) Mary is extraordinarily beautiful.

This is an example of the case in which an adverb is said to modify an adjective. How can such use of an adverb be reduced to the predicative use of an adjective? Admittedly, in this case, it has not yet been sufficiently clarified what would have to be taken as the syntactic base of the adverb. Some comments and suggestions will be made just to hint at a direction for further study of the problem in the future.

One can say that *extraordinarily* in (5) expresses the degree or extent of Mary's beauty. Thus, as a direct extension of what has been done above, one might relate (5) to

(35) Mary is beautiful to an extraordinary extent.

or

(36) The extent to which Mary is beautiful is extraordinary.

To be sure, this would reduce the adverbial use of *extraordinary* to the predicative use. However, these solutions do not seem to be syntactically satisfactory. While in the preceding cases the manner adverbs are presumably a primary constituent of the sentence, *extraordinarily* in (5) modifies *beautiful*, and together they constitute a constituent of the sentence. In fact, replacement of *to an extraordinary extent* in (35) by *extraordinarily* does not yield (5).

Note further that adverbs like *unbelievably,* which may be used as sentence adverbs but not as manner adverbs (although phrases like *in an unbelievable manner* are acceptable), can modify an adjective just as *extraordinarily* does. For example,

(37) Mary is unbelievably beautiful.

This, of course, is not paraphrased by

(38) Unbelievably, Mary is beautiful.

---

[7]In brief, it is contended that (34) does not reflect its base structure, the base form of (34) being assumed to be "That Mary danced in the manner in which Mary danced was unbelievable."

Here, the adverb *unbelievably* forms by itself a primary constituent of the sentence.

What should then be assumed to be the base form from which (5) is derived? The difficulty in answering this question seems to lie in the simple fact that our understanding of the adjective itself and the syntactic structure of the simple predicative judgment of the form (6) is not yet sufficient.

On a tentative basis, it may be suggested that the difference between the noun and the adjective in their basic syntactic and semantic role should not be exaggerated. Thus, for example, the two forms *beauty* and *beautiful* are but two different manifestations of one basic entity according to the context. In brief, one may take the sentence:

(39) Mary is beautiful.

to be a manifestation of an underlying structure that may be suggested by a pseudo-sentence:

(40) Mary is of beauty.

Then, *extraordinarily* in (5) may first be related to the attributive adjective *extraordinary* in:

(41) Mary is of extraordinary beauty.

In the ultimate analysis the base structure of (5) would appear something like

(42) Mary is of beauty (the beauty is of an extent that is extraordinary).

10. In the preceding sections, the three major uses of adverbs of the form *adjective* + *ly* have been dealt with, and they have been reduced basically to the predicative use of the corresponding adjective. Can this reduction be carried out for all instances of adverbs formed from adjectives with the suffix -*ly*?

First of all, there are obvious exceptions like *mainly*, *chiefly*, and *wholly*, simply because the words *main*, *chief*, and *whole*, although they are called adjectives, cannot be used predicatively. To understand how these adverbs are related syntactically and semantically to the corresponding adjectives, the syntactic and semantic nature of the latter must first be clarified. In fact, these adjectives have their own characteristics, besides their ineligibility for predication, and actually may not properly be called adjectives. For example, *the whole group* may be paraphrased by *the whole of the group*, and this may indicate a similarity between *whole* and such words as *all*.

Secondly, adverbs are sometimes found used with less distinct meaning. The adverb *basically* in the first sentence of this section would be such an example. The intended meaning would perhaps be something like *in the basic analysis* or *in the analysis of the basic structure*. It is interesting to observe that one can take advantage, so to speak, of the morphologic process of the *-ly* suffixation to express oneself somewhat vaguely. But that one can do so does not lend any support to the claim that *-ly* suffixation may represent another primitive type of formation of thought. It is obviously futile, however, to try to deal with all cases of adverbs with the suffix *-ly*, including cases like the above, by means of more or less uniform syntactic machinery.

Finally, however, there are still many instances of adverbs with the suffix *-ly* whose meaning is distinct, but which cannot be analyzed in any of the ways we have discussed. Those that serve as time adverbials are good examples. For example,

(43) Mary dances frequently.
(44) Mary will dance shortly.

These sentences may be paraphrased by

(45) Mary dances on frequent occasions.
(46) Mary will dance after a short interval (*or* after a short duration of time).

To test the general validity of the claim that adverbs with the suffix *-ly* can be semantically reduced to the predicative use of the corresponding adjective, one must examine each adverb and see whether or not it may be paraphrased by means of an appropriate preposition and a noun modified by the corresponding adjective. This would lead to an exhaustive study of adverbs and adverbial phrases in general.

Our present study ends here, with the opening of the general semantic question. It would seem safe to presume that the answer to the general question is, at least, almost affirmative; that is, in the last analysis, the exceptions, if any, to the general claim would not be many. However, how much syntactic generalization would follow from the semantic claim is another question. Take, for instance, (44) and its paraphrase (46); in (46) we may replace *short* by *long*, but not in (44).

But whatever the outcome of a more exhaustive semantic and syntactic study of adverbs, it would not invalidate the claim that the suffixation of *-ly* does not represent a primitive type of formation of thought, nor the maximally uniform syntactic account of adverbs of the types dealt with earlier in this paper.

Bibliography

CHOMSKY, NOAM. *Cartesian Linguistics*, New York: Harper and Row, 1966.

KATZ, JERROLD J. and PAUL M. POSTAL. *An Integrated Theory of Linguistic Descriptions*, Cambridge, Mass.: M.I.T. Press, 1964.

KURODA, S.-Y. (forthcoming) "Remarks on English Manner Adverbials," in *Studies in General and Oriental Linguistics*, a volume dedicated to Professor S. Hahori, eds. R. Jacobson and S. Kawamoto, Tokyo.

LAKOFF, GEORGE. "On the Nature of Syntactic Irregularity," Report No. NSF-16, the Computation Laboratory of Harvard University, 1965.

The Next Step: Suggested Readings

This is a minimal reading list. More advanced material is mentioned in the footnotes for each article as well as in the books listed below. Within sections the books are arranged in order of increasing difficulty.

Syntax

JACOBS, RODERICK A. and ROSENBAUM, PETER S. *Transformations, Style, and Meaning.* Lexington, Mass.: Xerox College Publishing, 1971.

JACOBS, RODERICK A. and ROSENBAUM, PETER S. *English Transformational Grammar.* Lexington, Mass.: Xerox College Publishing, 1968.

CHOMSKY, NOAM. *Syntactic Structures.* The Hague: Mouton, 1957.

O'BRIEN, R.J., ed. *Report of the Twenty-Second Annual Round Table Meeting on Linguistics and Language Studies.* Washington, D.C.: Georgetown University Press, 1971.

Phonology

SCHANE, SANFORD. *Phonology.* Englewood Cliffs, N.J.: Prentice-Hall, 1971.

Historical Linguistics

KIPARSKY, PAUL. "Linguistic Universals and Linguistic Change" in *Universals in Linguistic Theory.* New York: Holt, Rinehart & Winston, 1968.

Stylistics

JACOBS, RODERICK A. and ROSENBAUM, PETER S. *Transformations, Style, and Meaning.* Lexington, Mass.: Xerox College Publishing, 1971.

FREEMAN, DONALD C., ed. *Linguistics and Literary Style.* New York: Holt, Rinehart & Winston, 1970.

General Interest

BOLINGER, DWIGHT. *Aspects of Language.* New York: Harcourt Brace Jovanovich, 1968.

LYONS, JOHN. *Introduction to Theoretical Linguistics.* Cambridge, England: Cambridge University Press, 1968.

A B C D E F G   7 6 5 4 3 2